On Compassion, Healing, Suffering, and the Purpose of the Emotional Life

READING AUGUSTINE

Series Editor:
Miles Hollingworth

Reading Augustine offers personal and close readings of
St. Augustine of Hippo from leading philosophers and religious
scholars. Its aim is to make clear Augustine's importance to
contemporary thought and to present Augustine not only
or primarily as a pre-eminent Christian thinker but as a
philosophical, spiritual, literary, and intellectual icon of the West.

Volumes in the series:
On Ethics, Politics and Psychology in the Twenty-First Century,
John Rist

On Love, Confession, Surrender and the Moral Self,
Ian Clausen

*On Education, Formation, Citizenship and the Lost Purpose
of Learning,* Joseph Clair

On Creativity, Liberty, Love and the Beauty of the Law,
Todd Breyfogle

*On Consumer Culture, Identity, the Church and the Rhetorics
of Delight,* Mark Clavier

*On Agamben, Arendt, Christianity, and the Dark Arts
of Civilization,* Peter Ivar Kaufman

On Time, Change, History, and Conversion,
Sean Hannan

On Compassion, Healing, Suffering, and the Purpose of the Emotional Life

Susan Wessel

BLOOMSBURY ACADEMIC
NEW YORK • LONDON • OXFORD • NEW DELHI • SYDNEY

BLOOMSBURY ACADEMIC
Bloomsbury Publishing Inc
1385 Broadway, New York, NY 10018, USA
50 Bedford Square, London, WC1B 3DP, UK

BLOOMSBURY, BLOOMSBURY ACADEMIC and the Diana logo are
trademarks of Bloomsbury Publishing Plc

First published in the United States of America 2020

Cover design by Catherine Wood
Cover image © Shutterstock

A catalogue record for this book is available from the British Library.

A catalog record for this book is available from the Library of Congress.

ISBN: HB: 978-1-5013-4453-4
        PB: 978-1-5013-4452-7
        ePDF: 978-1-5013-4455-8
        ePUB: 978-1-5013-4454-1

Typeset by Integra Software Services Pvt. Ltd.

To find out more about our authors and books visit www.bloomsbury.com
and sign up for our newsletters.

CONTENTS

ACKNOWLEDGMENTS

I am grateful for comments from Alexander Alexakis, Sara Ellenbogen, and Jonathan Gaworski. I am also grateful to series editor Miles Hollingworth for his comments and encouragement throughout the process.

ABBREVIATIONS

Aesch., *Ag.*	Aeschylus, *Agamemnon*	*Agamemnon*
Ambr., *De offic.*	Ambrose, *De officiis ministrorum*	*On the Duties of the Priesthood*
De vid.	*De viduis*	*On Widows*
August., *C. acad.*	Augustine, *Contra Academicos*	*Against the Academics*
C. Faust. Man.	*Contra Faustum Manichaeum*	*Against Faustus the Manichaean*
C. Iul.	*Contra Iulianum*	*Against Julian*
Conf.	*Confessiones*	*Confessions*
De beat. vit.	*De beata vita*	*On the Blessed Life*
De civ. D.	*De civitate Dei*	*City of God*
De d. anim.	*De duabus animabus*	*On Two Souls*
De doct. Christ.	*De doctrina christiana*	*On Christian Doctrine*
De don. persev.	*De dono perseverantiae*	*On the Gift of Perseverance*
De Gen. ad lit.	*De Genesi ad litteram*	*The Literal Meaning of Genesis*
De Gen. c. Man.	*De Genesi contra Manichaeos*	*On Genesis against the Manichaeans*
De mor. Eccl. cath.	*De moribus Ecclesiae catholicae*	*On the Morals of the Catholic Church*
De mus.	*De musica*	*On Music*

De nupt. et conc.	*De nuptiis et concupiscentia*	On Marriage and Concupiscence
De Trin.	*De Trinitate*	On the Trinity
De util. cred.	*De utilitate credendi*	On the Profit of Believing
De ver. rel.	*De vera religione*	On the True Religion
Div. quest.	*De diversis quaestionibus*	On 83 Different Questions
En. in Ps.	*Enarrationes in psalmos*	Expositions on the Psalms
Ep.	*Epistulae*	Letters
In Evang. Iohan.	*Tractatus in Evangelium Ioannis*	Tractates on the Gospel of John
In Iohan. ep.	*In Ioannis epistulam ad Parthos tractatus x*	Homilies on 1 John
Retract.	*Retractationes*	Retractations
Serm.	*Sermones*	Sermons
Cic., *Att.*	Cicero, *Epistulae ad Atticum*	Letters to Atticus
Nat. D.	*De natura deorum*	On the Nature of the Gods
Tusc.	*Tusculanae disputationes*	Tusculan Disputations
De or.	*De oratore*	On the Orator
Fin.	*De finibus bonorum et malorum*	On the Ends of Good and Evil
Diog. Laert., *Vit. phil.*	Diogenes Laertius, *Vitae philosophorum*	Lives of the Philosophers
Epict., *Disc.*	Epictetus, *Diatribai*	Discourses
Eusebius, *Praep. evang.*	Eusebius, *Praeparatio evangelica*	Preparation for the Gospel
Hist. eccl.	*Historia ecclesiastica*	Ecclesiastical History
Gal., *De plac. Hipp. et Plat.*	Galen, *De placitis Hippocratis et Platonis*	On the Doctrines of Hippocrates and Plato

Gell., *NA*	Aulus Gellius, *Noctes Atticae*	*Attic Nights*
Geront., *Vit. S. Melan.*	Gerontius, *Vita Saint Melaniae*	*Life of Saint Melania*
Gregory Naz., *Or.*	Gregory Nazianzen, *Orationes*	*Orations*
Heb.	Hebrews	*Letter to the Hebrews*
Hippoc., *Loc. hom.*	Hippocrates (Polybus), *De locus in homine*	*On the Places in Man*
De nat. hom.	(ps.) *De natura hominis*	*On the Nature of Mankind*
Jer., *Ep.*	Jerome, *Epistulae*	*Letters*
Jn. Chrys., *De poen.*	John Chrysostom, *De poenitentia*	*On Penitence*
1 Jn	1 John	*First Letter of John*
Juv., *Sat.*	Juvenal, *Satyrae*	*The Satires*
Leo, *Serm.*	Leo the Great, *Sermones*	*Sermons*
Lk.	Luke	*Gospel of Luke*
Mt.	Matthew	*Gospel of Matthew*
Orig., *C. Cels.*	Origen, *Contra Celsum*	*Against Celsus*
Oros., *Hist. adv. pag.*	Orosius, *Historia adversus paganos*	*History against the Pagans*
Pelag., *Ep. ad Dem.*	Pelagius, *Epistula ad Demetriadem*	*Letter to Demetrias*
1 Pet.	1 Peter	*First Letter of Peter*
Phil.	Philippians	*Letter to the Philippians*
Pl., *Ti.*	Plato, *Timaeus*	*Timaeus*
Plotinus, *Enn.*	Plotinus, *Enneads*	*The Enneads*
Ps.-Andron., *De pass.*	Pseudo-Andronicus of Rhodes, *De passionibus*	*On the Emotions*
Prov.	Proverbs	*Proverbs*
Ps.	Psalms	*Psalms*

Rom.	Romans	*Letter to the Romans*
Sall., *Cat.*	Sallust, *De Catilinae coniuratione*	*The Cataline Conspiracy*
Salv., *De gub. D.*	Salvian, *De Gubernatione Dei*	*On the Governance of God*
Sen., *Clem.*	Seneca (the younger), *De Clementia*	*On Mercy*
Helv.	*ad Helviam*	*To Helvia*
Ir.	*De Ira*	*On Anger*
Tranq.	*De Tranquillitate animi*	*On the Tranquility of the Soul*
Stob.	Stobaeus, *Anthologion*	*Stobaeus, Anthology*
Test. Lev.	*Testament of Levi*	*The Testament of Levi*

1

Provocation

Compassion is the soul of Christianity. It is connected to every aspect of life, and its presence, or absence, shapes one's experience of the world. In support of this ideal, the Gospels record numerous instances of Jesus exercising compassion to heal those whose suffering he witnessed. Early Christian preachers urged their congregations to follow Jesus' example by compassionately embracing their fellow human beings and by providing the churches with the financial means to care for the sick and poor.

The acts of compassion that Christians are supposed to emulate never were merely the practical embodiment of an ethical obligation. They are in imitation and illustrative of the healings and exorcisms that Jesus performed to manifest the kingdom of God.[1] To be made aware of and to feel compassion for the suffering of others is to participate in Jesus' healing ministry and to witness the ushering in of his kingdom. When carried out appropriately, compassionate emotions have the potential to alter the fabric of the cosmos. The feelings and actions that are the consequence of identifying with the suffering of another human being signal the power of God breaking through the evil aspects of the world and the demonic taking flight.[2]

The Graeco-Roman Context

Christians were not the only ones in antiquity busy with the possibilities for compassionate healing. The Greek god of medicine, Aesclepius, the philosophers argued, was one such divine power that offered the healing of body and soul to those who slept in his temples. Inscriptions and statues testify that those seeking cures brought gifts and even consecrated their lives to him as to a god and savior. The cult that bore his name presented enough of a challenge to Jesus' ministry that the early Christians disputed the source and purpose of its powers. While Origen of Alexandria (d. *c*.253) conceded that a demon named Aesclepius healed physical ailments, he cautioned those impressed by the healings that "the cure of bodies is impartial, as it is a characteristic not only of the good, but also of the wicked."[3] The quarrel lay not with the cult's potential to effect legitimate healing, but with its moral insignificance and its apparent demonic inspiration. One of the early Christians' harshest critics, the neoplatonic philosopher Porphyry (d. *c*.305), agreed that healing was not evidence, in and of itself, of divine operation. Rather than healing the body, the aim of philosophy was the salvation of the soul. Like many of the ancient Greeks before him, he imagined salvation only for the souls of the intelligent and just.

This is precisely where the early Christians distinguished themselves from the preoccupations of the pagan world. Unlike the pagan healers who had little interest in the underclass of Roman civilization, Jesus came into the world to heal the broken, the outcasts, the sick and injured, the destitute, and the downtrodden whose physical and economic condition set them apart from society and excluded them from participating in religious life. Jesus acknowledged the ravages of, and then compassionately healed, human misery in all its forms. As a physician for the body, he healed its material suffering; as a physician for the soul, he restored its moral integrity and relationship to God. Both types of compassionate healing were accomplished, in the course of his ministry and by his death on the cross, without Christianity ever being defined primarily as a healing religion.

The cult of Aesclepius, in contrast, was such a cult of healing. It had little interest in examining the social and religious dimensions of its cures and even less interest in the interior moral life of its clients. In spite of the competition that such cults posed for the emerging church, or perhaps even because of it, there was "little attempt to exploit for apologetic purposes specific instances of Christian healing in an age in which testimonies to miraculous cures by pagan gods were common."[4] Though pagan opponents to the faith would claim that the magic of such men as the Greek philosopher Apollonius of Tyana (d. *c*.100), and the Latin rhetorician and philosopher Apuleius (d. *c.*170), was greater than the miracles performed by Christ, there was a certain reluctance to engage with such objections head on.[5] Christianity was not simply one healing cult among many in the Roman world. To present its cures alongside those offered by the pagan gods would have rhetorically undermined the uniqueness of its mission. In this regard it was better to leave well enough alone. Physical healing was the consequence, rather than the focus, of the Christian ministry. It was the visible and material manifestation of God's kingdom breaking through the evil rulership of this world.

The perception of power among the early Christians differed from that of their pagan counterparts who participated in healing cults. Whereas the pagans perceived power in terms of the present social hierarchy they submitted to, the early Christians were more rebellious. Inspired by the eschatological reversals of Jesus' ministry—where "the last will be first and the first will be last"— they recognized fluid relationships of power between "the haves" and "the have nots," between the elite and those excluded from ordinary social life, between the observer of human suffering and the sufferer.

Christian healing took place amid the larger theological questions that these reversals of the power structure posed for the spiritual life of ordinary Christians. From the stories the Gospels told, they noticed that the physical suffering of the body was only part of what Jesus had healed. They saw how Jesus had reintroduced social and religious outcasts, including the abject poor and the lepers, into the sacramental life of the church. He had also renegotiated the boundaries between human experience and divine sovereignty by encouraging people to consider what it meant to have been made in the image of God.[6] And by challenging them to examine the quality and intent of their moral decisions, he prioritized the interior dimension of their spiritual life and ethical commitments.

A further difference was in the conviction that the source of Jesus' power was God and that its purpose was the eradication of the demonic entities that wreaked havoc upon, and of the evil that ruled, this world. I have already suggested that the miraculous healings, which often reexamined social and religious norms, were a manifestation of the kingdom of God. The early Christians sensed that the healing of the physical body would not suffice to prepare them for the social, spiritual, and moral reversals that the presence of God's kingdom implied. It required a deeper examination of their interior motivations and of their experiences with respect to human suffering and to the ways in which such suffering mirrored and related to Christ's suffering on the cross.

In the light of this developing and multifaceted examination of their interior world, the early Christians wondered how they were supposed to connect with, experience, and react emotionally to the suffering they witnessed. Preachers responded with sermons encouraging a passionate connection with human misery. Jesus in his ministry had, after all, modeled such a connection. The Gospels record several instances of his feeling empathy for the people he had miraculously cured. Likewise, his agony in the Garden of Olives and his subsequent death on the cross were felt compassionately and on behalf of human suffering.

This was in contrast with the legacy Greek and Roman pagans had left with respect to the emotional dimensions of pity and its application across societal boundaries. The contexts in which pity could be legitimately expressed were in the social, rather than the emotional, structures and relationships between and among human beings. It was appropriate to feel pity for those among the upper classes who had experienced a sudden reversal of fortune, but not for the members of the lower classes in need of charity.[7] Among the pagans, pity reinforced social boundaries, rather than challenged them. Gary Ferngren has remarked, "pity was shown by those who, on the one hand, could sympathize with members of their own class in need and, on the other, might hope to build up a fund of good will in case they should experience a similar misfortune."[8] It is worth noting that the operation of such ideals did not prevent individual pagans from feeling pity for the suffering they witnessed, only that the emotional experience was neither normalized nor encouraged.[9] With no one among the literary elite committed to articulating the individual and emotional dimensions of pity, there was no explicit Greek and Roman tradition for the early Christians to draw upon.

The Jewish tradition was more fertile in this regard. For example, the Greek-speaking Jewish historian Josephus (37 CE–c.100 CE), like the Hellenistic historians of his day, explored the emotional aspects of the lives he recounted in his histories. He explained the actions of characters by their emotions, he portrayed characters according to the way they handled emotions, he interrupted the narrative to reflect upon emotional experiences, and he considered which emotion an event should provoke.[10] The anonymous *Testament of Zebulun* (1st–2nd century CE) deepened this exploration of emotional experience by considering how Zebulun—the last son of the biblical patriarch Jacob—responded to the suffering he witnessed. We are told that he distributed the fish he caught among strangers, prepared it for those in even greater need, and offered garments to a man he found naked in the winter. In all cases, his actions are described as compassionate, in some cases they involve the empathy of shared grief, and they are always rewarded with God's beneficence.

The early Christians received and developed this tradition of compassionate suffering in the context of Jesus' ministry. From the book of Genesis they knew that human beings were made in the image of God; from the Gospels they knew that this included the sick, the destitute, and the outcasts of Roman society. Early Christian preachers drew upon this unequivocal truth to motivate their congregations to perform charitable acts and to engage directly and emotionally with human suffering. In this regard they were unique.

While the ancient Greeks performed charity, it was based upon civic notions of virtue, rather than the innate dignity of the human person. The Stoics differed from the ancient Greeks in acknowledging an intrinsic humanitarian impulse that was grounded in reason and that distinguished human beings from the beasts.[11] Yet such universal values did not promise the reversal of well-entrenched social norms. According to Marcia Colish, one such advocate of the principles of a Stoic humanitarianism, the Roman satirist Juvenal contained "his egalitarianism and fellow-feeling...within certain elastic limits marked off by class, nationality, and sex."[12] Early Christian preachers challenged their congregations to reconsider such artificial boundaries when contemplating the appropriateness of compassionate feeling across the range of human suffering.

Emotions and Meaning

Among the early Christians, Augustine was especially adept at examining and articulating the interior life of the Christian in the context of compassion, healing, and suffering. He knew that feeling compassion for human suffering results in acts of charity and understanding that imitate the boundless love of God. This connection between feeling and charitable action generates all sorts of possibilities for spiritual transformation in the encounter between God and human beings. When attuned to the right frequency, unencumbered emotions serve as the gateway from this world to the next. The spiritual healing that takes place in the course of this transmission is what we call salvation.

This chapter will follow Augustine's emotional life from his early years as an auditor among the Manichaeans, to the emotional provocation he experienced while reading pagan literature and attending the theater, to the divinely chiseled emotions he felt while reading the Psalms. Over the course of this trajectory, Augustine learned that emotional experiences did not always need to be suppressed. Under the right circumstances, they could be spiritually transformative. For Augustine, this is especially the case when feelings of compassion or distress prompt people to call upon God, in this way triggering the conditions that make salvation possible.

Like the unfiltered, and sometimes unpredictable, emotions Augustine studied, his path toward understanding the nuances of emotional provocation did not progress in a linear manner. Reflecting upon the pain of personal loss and the challenge of spiritual conversion helped Augustine reassess the meaning he assigned to his emotional life over the course of time. Emotions were not merely unwelcome feelings that needed to be suppressed. When focused in the right direction and on the appropriate object, they could be transformed into alignment with the compassionate love of God. The process of reflection helped him reinterpret and then integrate past experiences and emotions into his developing sense of himself as a Christian. With the shifting landscape of his self-understanding he came to realize that we, as human beings, could know and see ourselves only in relation to God. The insight led to a renewed sense of optimism for the possibility of human transformation.

It might seem odd to use the word "optimism" to describe a man who believed that people were born with the corrupted nature he called original sin. Augustine knew that Adam's free will and pride had led to his disobedience in the garden and then to the stain of original sin. Humanity inherited not only the stain but also the guilt of Adam's transgression. A sense of remorse was, therefore, built into the human condition. Augustine was grappling with this remorse when he pondered the spiritual significance of his emotional life and of his response to human suffering. In the light of Adam's guilt, feelings of remorse, sorrow, and pain—what Augustine would have called *dolor* and *miseria*—were intrinsic to the examined Christian life.[13] The question was not whether to feel remorse, sorrow, and pain, but how to contextualize and give legitimacy to such feelings in a well-lived, morally rich existence. His sense of optimism resided in the assurance he ultimately won that feelings formed in virtue and sanctified by Christ become the bridge between lived experience and divine life.

Challenges of Manichaeism

When Augustine was a young man his optimistic drive resided elsewhere. It was the drive to uncover a distinctly articulated truth. He had been studying advanced rhetoric in Carthage in his later teen years when he read *Hortensius* for one of his classes. No longer extant, the book by the Roman statesman and philosopher Cicero (d. 43 BCE) urged its readers to control and monitor the passions in order to achieve the emotional equanimity that was the aim of the philosophical life. Excited, motivated, and inspired, Augustine described the emotional thrill of engaging with wisdom directly, rather than being bound by the limited truths of "this or that sect."[14] As moved as he was by this encounter with truth, he recalled some thirteen or fourteen years later that at the time of reading the *Hortensius* he was still distracted by "a fog" that obscured his path, and then by error, as he gazed up at "stars that plunged into the ocean." Though the young Augustine had indeed been interested in astrology, the stars he spoke of were a metaphorical allusion to the "men who held that the light that is seen with our eyes is regarded as being worshipped as the utmost divinity."[15]

He was speaking of the Manichaeans. They had convinced him that his novice Christian faith was based on the "terror of authority" rather than the "pure and simple reason" they promised to deliver.[16] Ready to clear the fog that obscured the path to comprehending truth, Augustine became a hearer among the Manichaeans, who, he thought, "taught rather than commanded."[17] We are left to conclude that he affiliated himself with the sect because they offered the reasoned certainties that his insecure biblical faith could not yet provide. Perhaps the sureness of their investigation had resonated with the same impassioned quest for truth that his encounter with Cicero's *Hortensius* had inspired.

There was more to the Manichaeans than their investigative method. Founded by the prophet Mani in third-century Persia, the sect was known for its cosmological dualism. Its followers believed that before the world began, light had existed independent of the darkness, until a cosmic struggle ensued that damaged the original integrity and forced an intermingling of the two principles. The creation of the material world was a fallen state that trapped particles of light with particles of darkness. Yet it was also the stage for redemption. This was where the descendants of Adam and Eve—that primordial mixture of light and darkness in its human form—labored in the body to bring about a cosmic separation. Elaborate food rites, practiced by elite members of the sect known as "the Elect," removed the light from the darkness and helped facilitate both a personal and a cosmic salvation. A strict regimen of disciplinary and alimentary practices formed the Manichaean self "by the '*gnosis* of separation,' the *practical* knowledge of discerning and marking apart a self amid the flood of passions and drives of the human body."[18] Jason BeDuhn has shown how a Coptic Manichaean psalm personified such passions and drives, imagining them as the external forces of a rebellious evil power acting upon receptive and pliable flesh.[19] A paradox of the sect was that the mechanisms of the material body, including the ingestion and digestion of light-trapped food, generated spiritual redemption.

One of the Manichaean doctrines the young Augustine may have been drawn to concerned the notion of evil. Embedded in the interrelationship between the principles of light and darkness, evil for the Manichaean was the result of outside forces acting upon the individual. In theory, the person who committed sin underwent an exterior struggle with a contradictory evil principle, rather than an interior conflict involving two opposing wills. The reality, however, was more complex, even as Augustine reported it in the various polemical contexts in which he encountered the Manichaeans. They, like Augustine, seem to have worried about preserving the unspoken laws of justice and accountability in such an ethical environment.

From his point of view, however, their dualistic system violated human freedom, no matter how hard they tried to avoid the insult. Sin, for Augustine, was the result of the will turning away from the good. Though human beings were born into sin, the freedom to fix this fallen state remained locked into the composition of the individual, made in the image and likeness of God.

Manichaean anthropology was different. It saw the human person as a lone actor on the cosmic stage, meant to use the material processes of the body as a way to separate light from darkness and overtake evil with the good. The inevitability of the cosmic drama, and the Manichaean's place in it, called the range and scope of human freedom into question. Augustine asked,

> Are they compelled to sin by being commingled with evil? If so compelled that there was no power of resisting, they do not sin. If it is in their power to resist, and they voluntarily consent, we must find out through their teaching why such great good things [reside] in supreme evil [and] why this evil [resides] in supreme good, unless it be that neither is that which they bring into suspicion evil, nor is that which they pervert by superstition supreme good.[20]

For Augustine, the exteriority of evil in their system was at the root of the difficulty. Sins that cannot be avoided are not sins; sins that we consent to cannot reside in a perfected nature. He reasoned that the light inhabiting the Manichaean body was not purely good, nor was the darkness invading it evil.

Everyday Evil

If the opposing forces of light and darkness do not govern our moral choices, then evil is something other than an internal conflict provoked by an external principle. An episode involving a theft of pears prompted Augustine's reexamination, some thirty years later, of the nature and causes of evil as it operates in our lives and shapes how we integrate ourselves along a continuum of moral options. Late one night he and a group of friends decided to steal some pears from a nearby orchard.[21] Looking back on the incident,

Augustine recalled that the pears were neither tasty nor appealing, and that most of what they stole they threw to the hogs. It was the theft itself that he had found alluring, the thrill of breaking the law in the company of like-minded friends. Yet there was more to the story than warning us, his readers, of the insidious threat of peer pressure generating senseless acts of moral depravity. The event revealed something unaccountable about the actions of evil, even something commonplace in its apparent insignificance. It dwelled in the trivial, waiting for its moment, nestled in mundane plans. The theft of the pears signaled to Augustine that evil, in its commonplace senselessness, settled into the unremarkable events of our lives.

When Augustine reflected upon the theft of the pears three decades later he understood how the Manichaeans had gotten the problem of evil wrong. In viewing evil as exceptional, they had distorted its routine nature and attributed its persistence in the world to external powers. Augustine's approach was different. Evil was not an uninvited, outside force imposing its will upon the goodness of our human predispositions. Nor could something so malevolent be assigned to an internal struggle of the will in conflict, the energetic offspring of opposing inclinations. Evil was absurd and paradoxical. Its nature being commonplace, but unpredictable nonetheless, it was likely to destabilize our self-understanding in ways we could not anticipate. It was contrary to every expectation and assumption about the direction of our emotional commitments and the nature of human longing.

Evil was mysteriously and paradoxically connected with love. This was how Augustine thoroughly assimilated the theft of the pears. It was a simple act of love for the crime, for the thrill of self-indulgence, for the pleasure of misguided company, for "the fault itself."[22] In the interim he had learned that sin was the result of desire aimed in the wrong direction, away from the sureness of God and toward the moral despair of materialism and emotional discontinuity. There was no conflict between the forces of good and evil, whether externally or internally imposed. Instead it was the direction of our aspirations—what we loved—that defined our moral choices. He now understood that we become what we love, even when we do not love what we have become. It meant that the self evolved in the context of love and along a continuum of ever more urgent decisions to love in this or that direction.

The Process of Emotional Refinement

When Augustine was a hearer among the Manichaeans he may
have been drawn to their understanding of disobedient human
emotions as something "alien to the self."[23] The advantage of this
way of thinking was its readiness to dismiss negative feelings and
experiences as an intrusion into a soul sublimely ordered and poised
to join the original integrity of the universal soul. Because there
was no interior drive to achieve equanimity, adverse feelings were
connected with the forces of darkness that opposed the glimmers of
primordial light. Consistent with this cosmic drama of separation
and restructuring, Manichaean love involved neither choice nor self-
determination. It was a static emotion synonymous with the Father of
the entirety, the Lord of totality, "who gave himself for everything."[24]
It was also "the beginning of all the righteousness and the divine
that dwells in the holy church." There was no ongoing decision to
love, only the original outpouring of divine beneficence mirrored in
the church. It did not need to be renewed, or provoked, or reflected
upon to achieve its ends. It simply existed as a wellspring of spiritual
generosity. "These two, the Mind and the church, a single body is
also their likeness; because, again, the apostle too shall give his own
self for his church. And again, due to this, the church too calls him
'love'." Its converse was "hate," "the first death that welled up... the
land of darkness... [that] ruined all its perdition's offspring... [and]
sinned even against a power foreign to it, and ruined it."[25] Because
Manichaean love was independent of choice, there was no need to
deliberate over the ethical circumstances of its allocation. It rejected
charity, insofar as giving "food to him who begs... [lets] the beggar
receive the light which is in food [and which] is a part of God, the
divine substance."[26] It was not flexible enough to encompass and
respond to the changing needs and desires of human beings.

For more than a decade Augustine accepted the uneasy comfort of
such a moral psychological framework. We do not know the extent
to which he struggled with the system privately, for the *Confessions*
recount his memories of the sect filtered through the critical lens
of revision and spiritual transformation. By the late 380s his
understanding of the psychology of the emotions had crystalized in
opposition to the Manichaeans. Now he could assert with confidence
that "the emotions of our mind are part of our nature. They are

nourished even along with us by knowledge of the finest rational and moral principles of eternal life, as if by the grain and the fruit-trees and the green plants."[27] Whereas the Manichaean view of such positive emotional states as love and generosity was connected statically to the eternal love of the Father of the Entirety, Augustine viewed them, almost paradoxically, as both embedded in our nature and cultivated in the context of the divine. Part of the natural composition of the person, emotions were not to be discarded as unwanted deposits on the soul. Nor should they be externalized and attributed to outside causes. With this aspirational view of our emotional life came certain responsibilities that the Manichaeans would have resisted, though perhaps not thoroughly rejected. Negative emotions were to be mastered by the virtues of temperance and modesty.[28] No longer in harmony with reason and with the drive for moral integrity, such mental states generated the disturbances of evil lusts and desires that Augustine called "perturbations."

The process of transforming such unruly passions into an obedience longing for righteousness was neither comfortable nor unassertive. It involved calibrating certain challenging emotions to fall into line with reason. "If [the emotions] are not harmonious and are managed negligently, they tear and destroy the mind, and make life miserable. Then they are called perturbations and lusts and evil desires. We have been commanded to crucify them in ourselves with all the energy we can until death is swallowed up in victory."[29] The effort involved in refining the maladies of the soul calls to mind a poem by Emily Dickinson (d. 1888), which dares us to witness "a soul at the White Heat." This is the point at which ore burns so hot that instead of burning orange or red it radiates the heat made visible into a glowing light. The transformation into incandescence, as it is called, happens, for Dickinson, under the pressure of the blacksmith's anvil, as it forges the "quivering substance" of the ore. "Least Village has its blacksmith/Whose Anvil's even ring/Stands symbol for the finer Forge/That soundless tugs—within—/." The work of the blacksmith invites us to consider the process of the soul's refinement not as something imposed from outside forces, as in the fires of hell, but as something generated, even more mysteriously, from drives and commitments within. The sheer effort of the soul bringing about this change continues "Until the Designated Light/Repudiate the Forge—" and the forge is no longer needed. For Dickinson, as for Augustine, the end of emotional refinement is the soul's purification.

When Augustine was in his early twenties he believed that emotional provocation could be pleasurable. It confirmed his sense of himself as formed uniquely by his experiences. At that point in time he did not see such provocation as something to be feared for igniting inappropriate drives at odds with sound moral determination. It was to be sought after and nurtured as a guilty pleasure. This sort of delight differed from the attitude that Jean-Jacques Rousseau (d. 1778), the philosopher of the French Enlightenment, cultivated toward the ebb and flow of emotional life. He envisioned its disturbances as being used beneficially to nurture compassion.[30] Witnessing, and even secretly delighting in, other people's pain was supposed to make us reflect upon the misery we have been spared, while at the same time reminding us of an uncertain future. The disparity between our circumstance and theirs—combined with the acknowledgement of our vulnerability—was supposed to stimulate compassion.[31] For the young Augustine, however, the emotional provocation allowed him to revel in other people's miseries without having to endure such hardships himself. He had yet to recognize the spiritual significance of shared emotions, only the perverse delight in exploiting them.

Investigating why vicarious feelings might be pleasurable was apparently foreign to the Manichaeans. Although they were ridiculed, perhaps unfairly, for showing an interest in their personal emotions, there is nothing to suggest that they found other people's emotions of any particular importance.[32] Augustine's fascination with shared emotional experiences, therefore, cannot be ascribed straightforwardly to his association with the sect. Perhaps it signaled his alliance shifting away from the emotional austerity of the Stoic wise man and toward the realization that virtuous emotions bridged the gap between the human and the divine. Between these limits of spiritual resolve stood the young Augustine, eager to feel secondhand miseries, yet unsure why.

Culture as Stimulus

The various dimensions of emotional provocation emerged in the context of his visits to the theater as a young man. He recalled that actors playing their parts had made him feel a kind of sorrow (*miseria*) that he had been familiar with, but would not have wished to experience directly. There was a curious pleasure he identified in sharing the actors' suffering. Yet he experienced this emotional contagion as a pretense that had no possibility of being converted into genuine misery. The theater allowed him to enjoy the emotion, while remaining detached from its consequences. The emotional safety of long-range suffering also figured prominently in the moral philosophy of Adam Smith, the economist and philosopher of the Scottish Enlightenment (d. 1790). In his theory of the judicious spectator, a rational observer places himself in our circumstances, studies our distress, and determines the range and scope of appropriate sympathy.[33] For Smith, the emotional distance created a dialectical engagement between the remote gaze of the observer and the self-involved misery of the sufferer. It served the moral purpose of soothing emotional distress.

For Augustine, there was no moral purpose in the vicarious emotion he felt at the theater. It was neither the *miseria* of individual, heartfelt suffering, nor the *misericordia*—the passionate compassion—of feeling the suffering of another human being. As he said concisely, the actors' feigned suffering provoked the feeling of pity, rather than the offer of assistance. Apart from the pleasure he felt, the feelings were morally pointless. "Yet he wants to feel from them sorrow (*dolor*), and the sorrow itself is his pleasure. What is this but a miserable madness?"[34] There was a danger, "a miserable madness," in feeling emotions simply for the sake of feeling them. Once the emotions had been provoked generally, there was the possibility of igniting further the immoral passions of lust and depravity.

It is striking that Augustine, in looking back at the time he spent at the theater, refused to reject passionate feeling. He saw his absorption in human emotion, even to the point of experiencing other people's pain, as a tolerable side effect of his desire to be compassionate. "Or, though no man is willing to be miserable, is he, nevertheless, pleased to be compassionate (*misericordia*), which because it is not without sorrow (*dolor*), for this reason alone are sorrows (*dolores*) to be loved?"[35] There was pleasure in sharing the misery the actors portrayed on the stage. He found no reason to reject this sympathetic identification with human suffering simply because the passionate feeling it stimulated could be diverted to such baser emotions as lust. The feeling was genuine, even though it was morally unstable. I recall that Emily Dickinson found pleasure in witnessing the pain of death because she knew the feeling was real: "I like a look of Agony,/Because I know it's true—/Men do not sham Convulsion,/Nor simulate, a Throe—/."[36] Whereas Augustine enjoyed the pleasure of shared experience, she was drawn to the authenticity of deathbed pain. Whereas Augustine seized the virtuous aspects of passionate feeling, and was willing to endure the moral ambiguity, she longed for the purity of the truth made known in the unfeigned misery of death. Whereas Augustine aimed for truth and regretted the futility of the stage, she seized truth in its morbid and unmitigated form.

Although Augustine did not eliminate compassion from his repertoire of emotional responses, he remained uneasy about the methods of its stimulation. As a boy in grammar school, he had been moved to tears by the death of Dido in the epic poem, the *Aeneid*, of Virgil (d. 19 BCE). With rapt attention he had read about the ghost of Creusa, the wife of Aeneas who was lost and then killed while fleeing the city, and about the wooden horse filled with armed men so instrumental in the subsequent burning of Troy.[37] Part of the grammar school curriculum, the study of Greek and Latin literature was treasured as an introduction to higher learning that surpassed the elementary lessons in grammar, reading, and writing. The ability to immerse himself in the pleasures of epic poetry would have been seen as an indication of his developing intellect. There is no suggestion that his grammar school teachers discouraged such emotional engagement as inappropriately sentimental. To the contrary, schoolboys learned to feel their sorrows and pains through such literary provocation.[38] They were asked to write prose summaries of passages from epic poems that elaborated upon certain emotions, whether grief or fear, appropriate to the speaker.[39] The problem for Augustine was not so much the emotive response as it was the literary fiction, the *poetica figmenta*, that caused it. Similar to the theater, epic poetry provoked real feelings with no moral substance. It left him alone with his sentiments to wander aimlessly through the emptiness of this life.

Augustine later identified such experiences as paradoxical rather than false. He had committed to memory the wanderings of Aeneas, though he had forgotten how he himself had been led astray; he had wept for the death of Dido, but had remained dry-eyed toward his own death with respect to God. Such feelings and commitments were misdirected as opposed to unseemly. It was appropriate to feel emotions deeply when reading the Bible and the Psalms,[40] but emotional discretion was required when reading pagan literature, which was, at best, morally ambiguous and, at worst, destructive. It was not necessary to stifle the emotional response to all literary experiences, but simply to read with an eye toward fostering moral commitments. The stories of lustful gods could be seen as offering schoolboys a model for their own sinful deeds, or as cautionary tales of moral failure to be avoided. Augustine distinguished the words that told such stories, which were "like vessels choice and precious," from the moral framework, the "wine of error," that his "intoxicated teachers" had poured into him and his classmates by the force of their will.[41] There was no need to reject the aesthetics of pagan literature when the possibility remained to sift it through the filter of a Christian cultural framework. Such was the work of Christian teachers.

The shortcomings of pagan literature paled in comparison to the fictional tales told by the Manichaeans. "How much better then are the stories of the poets and grammarians than these traps!...For I can turn a verse and a poem into true sustenance."[42] The tales of the Manichaeans were traps because they contained the name of Jesus Christ, but their "heart was devoid of truth."[43] The incongruity of their method had left Augustine with memories hardened into the coldness of disdain. It is true that the poets he had loved in his youth had also dazzled him with fictions. Unlike the poets, though, the Manichaean fictions had managed to deceive him, all while declaring "truth, truth." Their stories differed further from the poets in their studied disregard for emotional provocation. There was never a sense of fighting to repress any such passions stimulated by the idiosyncrasies of a Manichaean worldview. It was as if the promise of truth had stifled the affective response. In place of raw emotion, the apparent simplicity of their cosmological system temporarily filled a longing for order and clarity. Where there were questions—about the nature of evil and the structure of reality—the system provided ready answers.

If the poets left Augustine reeling with emotions that were perilously uncommitted to a Christian moral framework, then the Manichaeans left him emotionally dry and spiritually hungry for something more stable and true. He had mistakenly looked for

God among their stories, but had found himself undernourished and deceived in a way that differed from the godless fictions of epic poetry. Whereas the poets had enticed him away from God in his "gloomy desire (*in affectu tenebroso*)," the Manichaeans had seduced him with false hope.[44] It was an intellectual and spiritual, rather than a physical, seduction. "I happened upon that bold woman, without knowledge, a figure for Solomon, sitting at the door of her house and saying, 'eat hidden bread willingly and drink secret water that is sweet.'"[45] He had been drawn to the false reality, the promise of wisdom, the Manichaeans presented. Yet the emotional deception had been even subtler. It had promised that undesirable emotions were the product not of associations and experiences turned inward but of outside forces of darkness acting upon the unsuspecting person.

The Stoic Side

Augustine knew better than that. As a schoolboy he had been introduced to the moral psychology of the Stoics. They taught that four fundamental passions were the source from which all other emotions flowed. One such Stoic, Ps.-Andronicus (fl. 2nd–3rd century CE?), identified the passions as consisting of distress, fear, appetite, and pleasure. Though Augustine may not have known his work directly, it is worth quoting, because ideas similar to his were absorbed into the Graeco-Roman philosophical tradition.

> Distress is an irrational contraction, or a fresh opinion that something bad is present, at which people think it right to be depressed. Fear is an irrational aversion or avoidance of an expected danger. Appetite is an irrational desire, or pursuit of an expected good. Pleasure is an irrational swelling, or a fresh opinion that something good is present, at which people think it right to be elated.[46]

The sense of the "irrational" had nothing to do with the illogical or the absurd. It was in contrast to the Stoic view of nature as the perfected embodiment of "right reason," the so-called *orthos logos* that structures humanity and the world.

Later commentators, such as Galen, the physician from Pergamon, Turkey (d. *c*.200/216), connected the passions to certain deviations from an ideal natural operation of bodily systems within the human person. Passions, including the basic four listed above, were motions in one thing that came from something else.[47] Galen, for instance, distinguished the normal beating heart, which involved motion originating within the human body, from the heart experiencing palpitations, which resulted from an outside motion interfering with its normal function. The internal motion was valued as a natural activity synonymous with health, while the external motion, such as that involved in palpitations, signaled a negative passion. Because it was a problematic deviation from a natural physical process, it was something to be avoided and contained.

The same logic applied to emotional states, such as anger, which could be either an activity of the spirited part of the tripartite soul where it resided, or an external *pathos* that the rational part had failed to restrain. Stobaeus (fl. 5th century CE), a compiler of Greek prose, poetic, and philosophical works, confirmed the reception of such views into the fifth century: "[The Stoics] say that passion is impulse which is excessive and disobedient to the dictates of reason, or a movement of soul which is irrational and contrary to nature; and that all passions belong to the soul's commanding-faculty."[48] While Galen and the Stoics generally agreed that errant passions were the result of unnatural activities contrary to reason, their view differed significantly from that of the Manichaeans, who saw the passions as an interior expression of exterior evil unconnected to bodily processes. It was the difference between emotional distress due to the breakdown of internal reason, and emotional combat due to the cosmic opposition of light and darkness attacking the human person.

Like the Greek Stoics, Cicero built his moral psychology on the four fundamental passions of grief (*aegritudo*), joy (*laetitia*), fear (*metus*), and desire (*libido*). All the other passions he identified (in the *Tusculan Disputations*) formed subgroups within this framework.[49] The taxonomy of emotions he produced brought a sense of orderliness to the seemingly chaotic realm of thought and feeling that he and the Stoics called "disturbances of mind." The precision with which each emotion stood its ground in this moral psychological structure suggested, in Cicero's reading of the Stoics, "not only how faulty they are, but also the extent to which they are within our control."[50] Although he called them "disturbances," the passions were not outside forces acting upon an unwitting soul. They were rather the individual expression of our judgments and opinions. For Cicero, this meant that thinking and talking about our feelings helped regulate them.

There is nothing accidental about the way in which such passions relate to our life experiences. They are the affective manifestation of our perceptions and responses to the world. Grief, for example, is a recent opinion of the existence of a present evil; joy, a recent opinion of the existence of a present good; fear, an opinion as to an impending evil which seems beyond endurance; and desire, an opinion with regard to some good to come, which would be useful were it now present. While judgments and opinions form each disturbance, the disturbance—once it has arisen—produces further effects stemming from their existence in the mind. These effects can be either the gnawing pain of grief, the flight of the soul in fear, the merriment of joy, or the uninhibited craving of desire. If the original judgment and opinion form a weak assent to a disturbance emerging in the mind, then the subsequent effect solidifies the passion. The struggle to contain this emotional proliferation occurs in the soul, in which the wise man cultivates the virtue of equanimity, and to which everyone else applies a range of curative therapies.

Augustine subscribed to the Stoic theory of the four disturbances (*perturbationes*) of the soul, including desire (*cupiditas*), joy (*laetitia*), fear (*metus*), and sorrow (*tristitia*). Although his terminology differed slightly from Cicero's, he must have read the *Tusculan Disputations* during the course of his studies.[51] In doing so he had moved from the physicality of Cicero's *libido* and *aegritudo* toward the emotional suppleness of his own *cupiditas* and *tristitia*. The new terminology permitted the emotionally driven self-examination Augustine savored. In the light of the Stoic moral psychology with which he was familiar, it is difficult to imagine him having accepted unequivocally the Manichaean version of the same. There was a world of difference between emotional provocation taking place through sentient stimulation impacting the mind, and the model of involuntary assault envisioned by the Manichaeans. The former could be moderated by the equanimity of the wise man, which the masses emulated as an ideal, while the latter needed the practice of dietary rituals meant to benefit only the Manichaean elect.

Given that Augustine selectively appropriated the Stoics' moral psychology and rejected the Manichaeans', it is worth considering where he thought the emotions came from and how they should be triggered. We have seen that in his early years, while still an auditor among the Manichaeans, he fed his emotions on the drama of the stage and on the passions he read about in literature. There was nothing wrong intrinsically with culture generating emotion. The problem was that the lack of discernment had left him untethered emotionally. With no moral direction to steer him toward a path of spiritual transformation, he had no way of falling into line with the Stoics or of battling the darkness of the Manichaeans. Neither the equanimity of the Stoics, nor the emotional polarity of the Manichaeans would have explained the early life experiences, or responded to the challenges, Augustine described in the *Confessions*. There is no sense in which the Stoic quest for emotional equilibrium could have quieted the delight he felt while participating in the theft of the pears. Nor could the Manichaean opposition of good and evil have stopped him from experiencing the emotional lives of the characters he read about and witnessed on the stage. In reflecting on his past, Augustine was determined to show not simply that these approaches were morally wrong, but that they did not work. His emotional life was too rich to be silenced by a philosophical practice or dismissed by an ideology.

Reading the Psalms

In that case, halting the process of cultural and literary stimulation was not necessarily what Augustine had in mind. We have already seen that feelings triggered by pagan literature could be rendered spiritually beneficial when scrutinized through Christian eyes and sifted through a Christian cultural framework. Christian literature, in contrast, did not need a special lens through which to view its possibilities for spiritual nourishment. The sacred texts of the Bible and, in particular, the Psalms, abundant as they are in emotive language, offered fertile ground for generating a lively emotional response. Instead of quieting the emotions and stopping the spontaneous connection between reading a sacred text and feeling its emotional provocation, Augustine reimagined the significance of the affective experience by linking such emotions with God.

The Psalms, for Augustine, were the perfect literary vehicle for exploring such an emotional connection. A case in point is Psalm 49 [50], a liturgy of divine judgment: "Our God comes, he does not keep silent, before him is a devouring fire, round about him a mighty tempest/He calls to the heavens above, and to the earth, that he may judge his people/Gather to me my faithful ones, who made a covenant with me by sacrifice!/The heavens declare his righteousness, for God himself is judge!"[52] In Augustine's hands, the psalm is not simply about divine wrath. It is rather that God judges our righteousness by assessing our earthly commitment to care for the poor:

> The heavens have certainly announced this justice of God to us, for the evangelists have foretold it. Through them we have heard that some will be on the right hand, to whom the Master of the house will say, "Come, you whom my Father has blessed, receive." Receive what? The kingdom. In return for what? "I was hungry, and you gave me something to eat." What could be more insignificant, what could be more earthy, than to break bread with the hungry? Yet the kingdom of heaven values such things greatly.[53]

In the original psalm, the judgment of God threatened those who violated God's laws with fire and storms. For Augustine, the judgment that the psalm described was less about reprimand and correction than it was about motivation. Knowledge of the impending judgment of God inspired Christians to identify and carry out their moral obligations.

The possibility of judgment also encouraged people to ask God for help. In the words of Psalm 49 [50]: "Call upon me in the day of tribulation/I will deliver you, and you shall glorify me."[54] In Augustine's interpretation, caring for the poor was one such tribulation that prompted people to appeal to God. "We find wretched people for whom we show compassion; and the wretchedness of their miseries makes us feel compassion."[55] To the extent that witnessing other people's suffering provoked feelings of sorrow, it contributed to the experience of tribulation. The sense of unease and distress, which could not be healed on its own, encouraged people to align their priorities with God.

This meant that feeling pity and distress for other people's miseries served a purpose beyond that of alleviating their pain. It steered the content of an ongoing moral conversation Augustine was having about the meaning and purpose of suffering in our lives. Where the original psalm (49 [50]) asked God's people to call upon God in their tribulation, Augustine probed more deeply to ask why such tribulation was permitted at all. The question recalled the time he had spent as a Manichaean wondering about the nature of evil and the reason for its existence. The answer he found while studying the Psalms as a Christian connected the distress of tribulation with the productivity of emotional pain. For Augustine, experiencing one's own suffering, or identifying with someone else's, encouraged people to align themselves with God, in this way initiating the interior transformation that brings about salvation. As a legitimate expression of human suffering, painful emotions become the motivation by which, and the channel through which, people communicate their most heartfelt prayers to God.

There was no such teaching among the Stoics. They regulated emotional distress by distinguishing morally relevant states, such as virtues and vices, from neutral states that neither benefit nor harm a human being.[56] Emotional therapy for the Stoics consisted purely in cognitive modification that had nothing to do with opening an emotional gateway from this world to the next. The achievement of the Stoic wise man was his ability to discern that emotions, such as pleasure and pain, were among the life experiences that were neither good nor bad. Because such emotional states had nothing to do with the wise man's priorities, they had no significance for living the moral life.

Nor was there such a teaching among the Manichaeans. Although they had some interest in their personal emotions and were not above sharing them,[57] emotions were not thought to be of any spiritual benefit or consequence in the bodily rituals that separated strands of light from the darkness. Manichaean emotions did not connect followers of the sect with any kind of god.

Not all emotions felt by Christians were spiritually effective. To serve as a channel to the divine they had to be genuine. In the same Psalm 49 [50], Augustine warned of the man who suffered from tribulation, but then used it to call upon God in a routinized manner. The problem was that he had "grown slack about his prayer and let his fervor cool."[58] In the place of profound suffering, he had made the mere appearance of tribulation serve as a useful path to God. It was as if he sought out grief, and even the suffering of other human beings, for his spiritual gain. In Augustine's words, "he had become gravely infected by the corruption of his sins, and he had continued without feeling (*sine sensu*) and he found tribulation to be like a cauterization and surgery."[59] A habitual sinner, the man had replaced genuine emotion with his own utilitarian view of suffering, in which the pain of tribulation was controlled and then exploited.

Augustine believed that even the compassionate care of the poor could be distorted and misused when the mind of the caregiver had been spiritually compromised. Instead of looking for distress to alleviate, "How much better off you would be if you were in a country where you found no hungry person to feed, no wayfarer to be taken into your house, no ill-clad person to clothe, no sick person in need of a visit from you, no quarrelsome person to be reconciled with an opponent!"[60] It meant that feigning emotional distress, or provoking it unnecessarily, compromised the quest for virtue and the efficacy of prayer. It disrupted the affective pathway between the human and the divine.

The emotions, when provoked correctly, were connected with the process of spiritual healing, which always involved aligning the person with God. Made in God's image, all human beings were thought to be capable of cultivating the moral life so that the virtue of charity thrived. Understood as "the queen of all virtues,"[61] charity is the intercessor that "cuts through the air, surpasses the moon, exceeds the rays of the sun, and reaches the very heights of heaven … [until] it stands before the royal throne."[62] If charity is synonymous with love, and love is God,[63] then love is also the sum of the law in Christ: "For the entire law has been fulfilled in one statement, love your neighbor as yourself" (Gal. 5:14). Performing acts of charity joined the human with the vastness of the divine.

This was especially true for Augustine once the interior dimensions of charity were cultivated and accounted for. Charity was not simply an exterior performance of virtuous deeds. It had to be provoked by a genuine mind and heart and then accompanied by feelings of pity and mercy. Such feelings also had to be monitored and nurtured in the light of the possibilities for simulation and distortion. When experienced correctly, emotional provocation helped people identify with suffering in a way that fostered love and associated human experiences with divine love. It lessened the seemingly insurmountable chasm between the human and the divine.

There was no such possibility for emotional provocation as it was imagined among the Manichaeans. They were interested in opposing emotional assaults from outside forces and in personal emotions, if at all, merely for their own sake. Augustine must have seen the futility of such an emotional life. Charity existed among them only to serve the interests of the Elect and never to probe the suffering of other human beings. Healing consisted of elaborate rituals meant to separate elements of light from darkness and never to situate the person in relation to God. Likewise, the ancient Greeks performed charity to confirm civic notions of virtue, rather than expand upon the dignity of human beings. Although the Stoics acknowledged certain humanitarian principles, they fell short of overriding repressive social norms. For Augustine, the possibilities of emotional provocation challenged such assumptions, by connecting human beings to each other, and then by moving them along a charitable path that reached the heights of God.

Notes

1   Gary B. Ferngren, *Medicine and Health Care in Early Christianity* (Baltimore, MD: Johns Hopkins University Press, 2009), 62.
2   See Morton T. Kelsey, *Healing and Christianity: In Ancient Thought and Modern Times* (London: SCM Press, 1973), 58.
3   See Orig., C. Cels., 3.25.
4   Ferngren, *Medicine and Health Care*, 85.
5   See, for example, August., Ep., 136.1
6   Implicit in Jesus' ministry (Mt. 5:48), this is then combined with Gen. 1:27 and developed explicitly in patristic exegesis.
7   See Ferngren, *Medicine and Health Care*, 86, for a general discussion of pity in the ancient Greek world.
8   Ibid. 87.
9   Anneliese Parkin, "'You Do Him No Service': An Exploration of Pagan Almsgiving," in ed. Margaret Atkins and Robin Osborne, *Poverty in the Roman World* (Cambridge: Cambridge University Press, 2006), 70–71.
10 The list is from Françoise Mirguet, "Emotional Responses to the Pain of Others in Josephus's Rewritten Scriptures and the Testament

of Zebulun: Between Power and Vulnerability," *Journal of Biblical Literature* 133, no. 4 (2014): 838–857 (841).

11 Juv., *Sat.*, 6.

12 Marcia L. Colish, *The Stoic Tradition from Antiquity to the Early Middle Ages*, vol. 1 (Leiden: Brill, 1990), 223.

13 August., *De civ. D.*, 14.9: "For to feel no pain at all while we are in this place of misery truly takes place not without the great price of cruelty in the soul and of insensitivity in the body."

14 August., *Conf.*, 3.4.

15 August., *De beat. vit.*, 1.4, discussed in Serge Lancel, *St. Augustine* (London: SCM Press, 2002), 37 and 483, n. 1.

16 August., *De util. cred.*, 2.

17 August., *De beat. vit.*, 1.4.

18 Jason David BeDuhn, *The Manichaean Body in Discipline and Ritual* (Baltimore, MD: Johns Hopkins University Press, 2000), 227.

19 See BeDuhn, *The Manichaean Body*, 97.

20 August., *De d. anim.*, 12.18. Adapted from trans. Albert H. Newman, *On Two Souls, Against the Manichaeans*, in ed. Philip Schaff, *St. Augustine: The Writings Against the Manichaeans and Against the Donatists*. Nicene and Post-Nicene Fathers (=NPNF) 4 (Grand Rapids, MI: T&T Clark, repr. 1989), 105.

21 August., *Conf.*, 2.4; see James Wetzel, "Augustine," in ed. John Corrigan, *The Oxford Handbook of Religion and Emotion* (Oxford: Oxford University Press, 2008), 356–358.

22 August., *Conf.*, 2.4.

23 Jason David BeDuhn, *Augustine's Manichaean Dilemma, vol. 1: Conversion and Apostasy, 373–388 AD* (Philadelphia: University of Pennsylvania Press, 2010), 93.

24 Iain Gardner and Samuel N. C. Lieu, *Manichaean Texts from the Roman Empire* (Cambridge: Cambridge University Press, 2004), 252.

25 Ibid.

26 Ibid. 245.

27 August., *De Gen. c. Man.*, 1.20; trans. Ronald L. Teske, S. J., *Saint Augustine. On Genesis*. The Fathers of the Church 84 (Washington, DC: Catholic University of America Press, 1991), 79.

28 Ibid. 78.

29 August., *De Gen. c. Man.*, 1.20; adapted slightly from trans. Teske, *On Genesis*, 79.

30 Richard Boyd, "Pity's Pathologies Portrayed: Rousseau and the Limits of Democratic Compassion," *Political Theory* 32, no. 4 (2004): 519–46 (526).

31 Jean-Jacques Rousseau, *Émile* 4, trans. Barbara Foxley, *Émile* (London: Everyman, 1993), 228.

32   Josef Lössl, "Augustine's Confessions as a Consolation of Philosophy," in ed. Jacob Albert van Den Berg, Annemaré Kotzé, Tobias Nicklas, and Madeline Scopelio, "*In Search of Truth*": *Augustine, Manichaeism, and Other Gnosticism* (Leiden: Brill, 2011), 55.

33   Adam Smith, *The Theory of Moral Sentiments* (New York: Penguin Books, 2009), 1.1, 13. He defined pity or compassion as "the emotion that we feel for the misery of others, either when we see or are made to conceive of it in a very lively manner." Ibid. 1.4, 28.

34   August., *Conf.*, 3.2.

35   Ibid; see trans. William Watts, *St. Augustine's Confessions* 1 (Cambridge, MA: Harvard University Press, repr. 1942), 103. Note that *dolor* means not only "sorrow," but also "distress," "pain," "grief," "tribulation."

36   Emily Dickinson, "I like a look of Agony."

37   August., *Conf.*, 1.13.

38   Lössl, "Augustine's Confessions," 59.

39   August., *Conf.*, 1.17.

40   Lössl, "Augustine's Confessions," 59.

41   August., *Conf.*, 1.16; see Watts, *Confessions*, 49.

42   Ibid. 3.6.

43   Ibid.

44   Ibid. 1.17 and 3.6.

45   Ibid. 3.6, citing Prov. 9:13–17.

46   Ps.-Andron., *De pass.* 1, in A. A. Long and D. N. Sedley, *The Hellenistic Philosophers*, vol. 1 (Cambridge: Cambridge University Press, 1987), 411.

47   Gal., *De plac. Hipp. et Plat.*, 6.1.6.

48   Stob., in Long and Sedley, *Hellenistic Philosophers*, 410.

49   Cic., *Tusc.*, 4.

50   Ibid. 4.7; adapted slightly from trans. J. E. King, *Cicero: Tusculan Disputations*. Loeb Classical Library (=LCL) 141 (Cambridge, MA: Harvard University Press, 1945), 343.

51   August., *Conf.*, 10.14.

52   Ps. 49 [50] lines 3–6.

53   August., *En. in Ps.*, Ps. 49 [50].13; PL 36, 579; trans. Maria Boulding, O. S. B., *Expositions of the Psalms 33–50*, 3/16 (Hyde Park, NY: New City Press, 2000), 393.

54   Ps. 49 [50] line 15.

55   Ibid. 49 [50].22; PL 36, 579.

56   See, for example, Diog. Laert., *Vit. phil.*, 7, 101, discussing the Stoic philosopher Zeno.

57   Lössl, "Augustine's Confessions," 59.

58   August., *En. in Ps*, Ps. 49 [50].22; PL 36, 579; Boulding, *Expositions of the Psalms*, 400.

59 August., *En. in Ps*, Ps. 49 [50].22; PL 36, 579; adapted from Boulding, *Expositions of the Psalms*, 400.

60 August., *En. in Ps*, Ps. 49 [50].22; PL 36, 579; Boulding, *Expositions of the Psalms*, 401.

61 Leo, *Serm.*, 48.4, 13 March 455.

62 Jn. Chrys., *De poen.*, *hom.* 3, Patrologia Graeca (=PG) 49, 293.

63 1 Jn 4:8.

2

Sadness

Emotions configured properly along the tracks of charity, love, mercy, and joy move human experience gently toward divine intention. The challenge lies in coming to terms with baser life experiences triggering lower forms of self-expression, such as anger, envy, and untamed desire. In its broad outlines, the Graeco-Roman world of thought the early Christians drew upon followed similar expectations. Love and charity were considered good emotions the philosopher should strive for in their various manifestations, while anger was unhealthy and even unattractive. Widespread across time and place, anger was supposed to be diffused and controlled before its particular mode of irrationality deteriorated into a well of insanity, from which no reasoned line of thought could extricate its subject. Perhaps the Roman Stoic philosopher Seneca (d. 65 CE) said it best: "[With anger], the mind is driven by none more frantic nor susceptible to its own power, and, if it succeeds, by none more arrogant, or, if it fails, by none more insane."[1]

Augustine, like the other early Christians, differed from this assessment by degree, rather than kind. Even though the modulation of anger into something useful and manageable could generate the virtuous emotion of righteous indignation, it was generally better to refuse its entry into the realm of festering experience. Likewise, the dissatisfaction of envy could be used to invigorate action bringing about change; and desire could be altered by moving its object away from the insubstantiality of material longing and toward the eternal and ever-real longing for the divine.

Sadness was different from these other emotions. It was neither the virtuous feeling of love, nor was it counted among the dubious feelings that were supposed to be summarily rejected or, with the right cultivation, transformed into a beneficial version of the same. Echoing the vicissitudes of life itself, it was the inevitable expression of loss, disappointment, and unasked-for changed. To refuse the feeling of sadness would be like refusing the truth of one's existence in the material world. On this principle, the Graeco-Roman philosophers and the early Christians generally agreed. For the most part they thought that the expression of grief should be tempered, at times, with self-control. Where they differed was in the moral significance they assigned to such feelings.

To highlight the subtle variations between the philosophers, on the one hand, and the early Christians, on the other, it might be helpful to imagine sadness as an emotion understood along a continuum. At one end stands the Stoic philosopher, who tolerates sadness in the context of the wise man's quest for emotional control: he acknowledges its reality, while diminishing its relevance for the moral life. On the other end stands the early Christian, who easily equates sadness with human suffering and with the redemptive suffering of Christ on the cross. In this theological framework, sadness is not merely the result of life's vicissitudes, ebbing and flowing together with random encounters, but is part of a purposeful trajectory of the self, moving in harmony with God.

At various times throughout his life, Augustine stood on one or another point along this continuum. As a young man still enamored with the moral certainties that Manichaeism had promised to bring, he wrestled both with his persistent narcissism and with the futility of attaining the emotional tranquility of the Stoic wise man. Over time, he challenged this ideal in the context of personal grief and of his observations regarding the inevitability of human suffering. Finally, his rejection of Manichaeism, his ever more refined reception and reinterpretation of pagan philosophy, and his evolving commitment to see himself in the light of God shaped his experience and understanding of sadness into something distinctly Christian.

Definitions

Augustine used several words to signify "sadness," including *tristitia*, *maestitudo*, and *dolor*, each of which I shall examine here. In addition to "sadness," the word *tristitia* suggested "gloominess," "sorrow," "grief," and "melancholy," while its opposite was *laetitia*, meaning "joy."[2] *Tristitia* could also signify more than emotional suffering. It sometimes resulted from a spiritual challenge that the person whose "will" had been led in the wrong direction fell prey to. Note that, for Augustine, there was indeed a correlation between "will" and "emotion," in the sense that a right will (*voluntas*) is equated with good love and a distorted will with wrong-headed love.[3] Emotions that result from a well-directed love—whether desire, fear, or joy—are counted among the good emotions. Whether *tristitia* could be understood as one such good emotion was, however, philosophically ambiguous. As Augustine put it,

> with respect to sadness (*tristitia*), which Cicero prefers to call sickness (*aegritudo*), and Virgil pain (*dolor*), as he says, "they feel pain and joy," but which I prefer to call sorrow (*tristitia*), because sickness and pain are more commonly used to express bodily suffering—with respect to this emotion, I say, the question whether it can be used in a good sense requires more diligence.[4]

Augustine's use of the word *maestitudo*, which signified primarily what we mean by "sadness," was more straightforward than his use of the word *tristitia*. In contrast with *tristitia*, it did not imply the outward demeanor of sadness, denoted by such words as "moroseness" and "gloominess," but rather its interior sensations. To feel *maestitudo* was to experience authentic grief that touched the soul. It was not simply the exterior manifestation of grief as expressed through tears. Ambrose (d. 397), the bishop of Milan who baptized Augustine, used the word *maestitudo* to indicate the sadness that a widow feels profoundly. Although the feeling of loss was private, it was expressed publicly in the tears she shed for herself and, by extension, for the world: "The widow has, then, this excellent recommendation, that while she mourns her husband she also weeps for the world, and the redeeming tears are ready, which shed for the dead will benefit the living."[5] The moral value of her tears lay in making private experience public and in making individual grief meaningful for the world. It was not unlike Jesus' redemptive suffering on the cross. As the appropriate expression of inward grief, weeping stimulated compassion (*misericordia*), assuaged pain (*dolor*), reduced distress (*labor*), preserved the sense of propriety (*pudor*), and alleviated misery (*miseria*).

Augustine used the same word, *maestitudo*, to describe the intense emotional pain he felt when his mother, Monica, died: "I closed her eyes, and there flowed in my heart an immense sadness (*maestitudo*) and it overflowed into tears."[6] Whereas for Ambrose *maestitudo* was the heartfelt torment of private grief erupting into the public domain of self-expression, for Augustine the feeling was visceral. Whereas Ambrose recognized the moral possibilities inherent in the private becoming public, Augustine was circumspect. In his early years, as we shall see, he resisted such emotional displays of sadness as something shameful that he struggled to suppress.

The semantic range for the word *dolor* moves beyond the nebulous realm of "misery," as suggested by the words *tristitia* and *maestitudo*, to include the experience of physical, emotional, and spiritual pain. Unpleasant sensations in the body caused by illness and other physical trauma result in *dolor*, which can be converted into the mental suffering of "grief," "sadness," and "depression." *Dolor* can also be primarily emotional, resulting from disagreeable situations and experiences that leave the person feeling grief-stricken. When left unchecked, such feelings often degenerate into the spiritually impoverished state we call "despair." The contemporary perception of suffering also tends to collapse the distinction between physical and emotional manifestations of pain. We acknowledge that physical pain might result in feelings of grief, while the sorrow of depression might result in physical pain and other bodily ailments. Augustine connected body and mind in a way that was similarly reinforcing: "What is bodily grief (*dolor corporis*)," he asked, "but the sudden loss of health in something that the soul has made a bad use of, rendering it liable to corruption? And what is spiritual grief (*dolor animi*), but to lose mutable things that the soul enjoyed or hoped to be able to enjoy?"[7] In both cases, *dolor* is a loss that leaves the person feeling incomplete, so that either her physical or spiritual integrity has been compromised. "Instead of being able to enjoy the full vigour of perfection, animated being is afflicted by the evil of *dolor* and has to suffer privation."[8] As I shall confirm in Chapter 3, it follows that God and the angels do not feel *dolor*, because they are perfect being, with no possibility for integral loss or any other sort of essential change.

Engaging the Stoics

To explore the moral dimensions of sadness, Augustine reinterpreted Stoic philosophy according to his theology of good and evil and his philosophical understanding of the will in relation to it. In the context of such priorities he tells us that the Stoic philosophers permitted three good emotions to the wise man, and only to the wise man, namely "will" in place of "desire," "contentment" in place of "joy," and "caution" in place of "fear." "Will" seeks the good, "contentment" possesses a good that is appropriate to the wise man, while "caution" avoids evil. We are further told that Cicero called such states good emotions, or *constantiae*, which can be understood as "steadfastness" and "self-possession," while the Greeks called them *eupatheiai*, or "innocent emotions." Such feelings are permissible to the wise man because they, being positive, do not damage his tranquility. Caution, for example, differs from fear, because it circumvents the evil at the root of every wrong emotion, instead of reacting to it. In contrast with the wise man, fools are those who wallow in such unseemly emotions as "desire," "rejoicing," "fear," and "sadness," which Cicero referred to collectively as "perturbations" and the Greeks as *pathe*.[9] These so-called "passions" are bad emotions because there is something inappropriate and even appalling in their manifestation.

For Augustine, the difference between wise men and fools turned on an underlying notion of evil and on assumptions about where precisely evil is located and how it comes about. Evil is not an entity that exists independently and on its own terms. It originates in the quality of the will and of the love that provoked it. As Augustine put it, the right will is well-directed love, and the wrong will is ill-directed love; if well-directed love results in good emotions, then ill-directed love results in bad emotions.[10] Evil then thrives in the chaos of these bad emotions, which are reactions to events and situations brought about by a will that is headed in the wrong direction.

For Augustine, the Stoic practitioner tuned himself intellectually to circumvent this process. When bad things happened to the Stoic, he adopted the attitude of a fatalist. In life's calamities he recognized the futility of randomness because he did not have a stake in the unfolding of such events. The Stoic did not "take arms against a sea of troubles" because he knew that not "by opposing" would he "end them" but by adjusting and fine-tuning his mental commitments. There was no possibility of an emotional response to something the Stoic perceived as being disconnected from the movement of his will. Having oriented his will in the right direction, the Stoic detached himself from certain kinds of pain. As Augustine remarked, "But sorrow (*tristitia*) arises from evil that has already happened; and since they think that no evil can happen to the wise man, they have said that there can be nothing in his mind equivalent to sorrow."[11] The Stoic tempered, and even eliminated, his emotional reactions in the light of what he knew about himself in relation to the pointlessness of so many of the world's obligations.

For the Stoic philosophers who speak to us in their own words, such as Cicero and Seneca, life's unwelcome challenges were understood with a slightly different emphasis. In the core of his being, the wise man was someone whose primary commitment to moral excellence skillfully helped him avoid any such emotions that might subject him to the indignity of fluctuation. True virtue was rare, because life, from the outset, conspired to deceive. For instance, Cicero knew that in the course of our upbringing, we are subjected to deceptions so intricate that "truth gives way to falsehood and nature itself to fixed belief."[12] The spiritual error that resulted from this early deception burrowed deep into our desire for material gain and lust for pleasure. It produced the true sickness of the soul, the *insanus* or "unsound" mind, which required a special course of treatment to bring about a cure. The soul that had fallen into such desires (*cupiditates*) and accompanying distress (*aegritudo*) could be set on its proper track by detaching itself emotionally from outcomes it recognized as having nothing to do with the attainment of true moral virtue.

According to Cicero, the Stoic used his tranquil mind to navigate this web of deceit and align himself with truth. Social conventions were there to be exposed, not assented to uncritically. There was a difference, for example, between fake and genuine achievement. Fake achievement was the coveted prize of honor and reputation, which was really just an illusion that foolish men chased after in their dreams. Genuine achievement was the unbiased consensus of preeminent men with respect to moral excellence.[13] Its mode of operation was truth and its substance was real, not some "shadowy phantom" of the acclaim so many men desired. It had little to do with public office or military rank and everything to do with moral consensus about the content of virtue.

Likewise for Seneca, a rebellious soul could alleviate much of its distress by balancing the pitfalls of public life with the quietude of private introspection. The wisdom of reflection dissolved such harmful emotions as anxiety, sorrow, and fear by returning them to the context of their social manifestation.[14] Money, for example, was to be recognized as a source of suffering for rich and poor alike, "for their money has a fast grip on both and cannot be torn away without their feeling it."[15] People were supposed to understand that money was ephemeral and fostered greed. There was nothing inherently true about its worldly distribution. The Stoic having achieved emotional tranquility knew the difference between material things and occurrences of no significance to his moral flourishing and the primary, lasting virtues that really mattered. It wasn't what the Stoic loved, but what he knew to be the truth, that shaped his moral destiny. If Stoicism was a cognitive response to questions of virtue, then correct thinking resulted in the correct determination of what counted as a moral good.

With the eye of a critic, Augustine moved these doctrines of the Stoics into his theological framework. He found their method of rearranging social priorities unresponsive to the real truth about sadness (*tristitia*) and its mode of operation in our lives. In making such a change, Augustine reinterpreted the meaning of sadness and its relevance for virtue. As James Wetzel has remarked, "Augustine's rehabilitation of grief marks his profoundest break not only from the cognitive therapy of Stoicism but from all the various forms of philosophical self-help he associated with classical culture."[16] In addition, Wetzel has said, "Often, in fact, grief is the necessary and appropriate affective form of virtue. Augustine is clear in his use of the term 'grief' (*tristitia*) that more is at stake than the experience of unpleasant or painful physical sensations."[17] While still a young man, Augustine had taken Stoicism seriously enough as a philosophical system that he could not reject its findings with respect to sadness and grief without further comment. He credited Cicero's *Hortensius*, after all, with inspiring in him a love for the "immortality of wisdom." That such a love had steered him initially along a path toward Manichaeism did not mean necessarily that the truths of philosophy should be dismissed. He understood, like Basil of Caesarea (d. 379) before him, the relevance of the *disciplinae liberales*, which included pagan philosophy, for training the Christian mind. But as his time spent in the error of Manichaeism had shown him, for such an educational program to be useful, it had to be focused through the lens of a biblical worldview. It was not until his later years that Augustine envisioned a distinctly Christian course of study through which "a person could achieve rhetorical eloquence through ecclesiastical literature and wholly apart from the pagan classics."[18] In the meantime, the Stoic view of sadness and grief would have to be reassessed theologically, rather than rejected summarily.

Augustine addressed the Stoic repudiation of sadness, which Cicero called *aegritudo*, in *City of God* 14.8. I have already shown that sadness, in Augustine's view of Stoicism, was the result of an evil that had already taken place. Insofar as the wise man could not experience evil, he could not feel sadness. Note that Cicero had said that sadness was a kind of wrong-headed analysis about what constituted a moral good. In his words, "Distress (*aegritudo*) then is a recently formed belief of present evil, the subject of which thinks it right to feel contraction and dejection in the soul."[19] For Augustine, however, the Stoics viewed sadness as more a spontaneous reaction to the problem of evil than a reasoned opinion regarding its existence. To the extent that the wise man could not, due to his emotional tranquility, be triggered by evil, sadness became a morally meaningless impossibility.

The moral insignificance of Stoic sadness posed a problem for Augustine, both in the light of his experience and observations as a fallen man living in a fallen world, and in the light of what he knew about the suffering of Jesus during his ministry and on the cross. Whereas for the Stoic, sadness was an illusion based on an individual's perception of what truly mattered, for Augustine sadness had to be real and morally significant, because the distress was real. To deny the experience of sadness would be like denying that Jesus had suffered in the flesh and as a man. There was a word for those who had imagined such a placid and apathetic human life for Jesus. They were called "docetists" for their belief that Jesus' bodily existence had been a facade, devoid of reality. For Augustine, this rejection of human experience would have compromised the redemptive power of the cross.

The Example of Ambrose

Augustine was not the first to have reexamined the pagan philosophers' understanding of sadness (*tristitia* or *aegritudo*) and pain (*dolor*) in a densely imagined Christian setting. Before him, Ambrose quarreled with pagan philosophers who argued that freedom from pain (*dolor*) was necessary to partake in the blessed life.[20] Such philosophers, he said, contradicted the Gospel of Matthew, where those who had suffered the pain of persecution were counted among the blessed.[21] In acknowledging that such virtuous men as Moses and Job had experienced a meaningful kind of pain that was consistent with the blessed life, Ambrose destabilized the Stoic moral system. Pain was supposed to be cultivated in its own right, as an authentic expression of a life lived fully in the tragedy of the world. It was a legitimate path to virtue that did not need to be suppressed.

The importance Ambrose ascribed to pain is reflected in his revision of the Stoic model. The four Stoic emotions of pleasure, desire, grief, and fear were reduced to the same two emotions of pleasure and pain that Aristotle had articulated. In making this reduction, he acknowledged that pain was essential to the human constitution. It was a fundamental emotion that was "part of the human being's God-ordained design."[22] For Ambrose, its moral significance was confirmed by the vividness of Christ's experience on the cross, the suffering of the martyrs, and the pain endured by the great biblical figures from the past.

> Let there be something bitter in these sufferings, a pain that strength of mind cannot hide. Neither should I deny the sea is deep because the coast is shallow, nor that the sky is clear because sometimes it is covered with clouds, nor that the earth is fruitful because in some places there is barren ground, nor that the crops are fertile because they sometimes are mixed with sterile weeds. Likewise, consider the harvest of a blessed conscience to be mingled with some of the bitterness of pain (*dolor*).[23]

It would be disingenuous to cut pain off from participating in the variety of emotions that constitute a human life. Under the right conditions, a lively, and even painful, emotional experience could be an expression of virtue. Whereas the Stoic philosophers had found little of value in the range of emotional experience, Ambrose saw there the potential for moral progress and spiritual insight.

Personal Loss

From all the emotions Augustine could have felt, it was *dolor* that overwhelmed him when he, as a young man, lost his friend. To understand why, it is necessary to recount the episode in some detail. Augustine was twenty years old when he returned to his hometown of Thagaste to teach grammar, probably under the patronage of the same wealthy friend, Romanianus, who had financed his training in rhetoric some years earlier.[24] As Serge Lancel has remarked, "The township offered no future to an ambitious young man, but life probably drifted on fairly pleasantly, warmed especially by friendships."[25] In addition to Romanianus, Romanianus' son Licentius, and Alypius (the last two of whom would later accompany Augustine to his philosophical retreat at Cassiciacum, Italy), these friendships included the unnamed young man he had known as both a schoolmate and playmate. As Augustine tells it, their friendship was strengthened by a shared commitment to the Manichaeism that Augustine had introduced him to. It was an admission of guilt that absolved his friend of responsibility for their wandering ways.[26]

It is significant that Augustine never reveals the name of his friend. This is probably because the friendship was based on the lie of Manichaeism and never rose to the level of a friendship bound by the love of the Holy Spirit. He did not name his friend because the friendship was not true in the Christian sense of the word and, therefore, did not merit being named. Described as *dulcis*, the friendship was characterized by its pleasantness and agreeability, nurtured, as it were, by the enthusiasm they held in common for the "superstitious and pernicious fables" of Manichaeism. It continued along these lines—"sweet beyond all sweetness"—for approximately one year, until his friend became seriously ill with a fever. Close to death, he received baptism, though without his consent. When he emerged briefly from his fever, Augustine attempted to mock the baptism he knew his friend had received while unaware of what was happening to him. Much to his surprise, his friend was outraged; he warned Augustine to stop such talk if he wanted to continue the friendship. A few days later, the fever returned and his friend died. He died as a Christian.

Augustine described the grief he felt—the *dolor*—as a profound sense of emptiness and emotional pain. "Everywhere I looked was death. My hometown was a punishment to me, and my father's house a strange unhappiness, and whatever I had participated in with him turned into an immense torture without him."[27] In agony, he was empty and longing for a fleeting type of fullness he remembered just enough to taunt him. This sort of longing aggravated his pain, as he recalled his friend's presence along the well-worn tracks of his mind. Searching in vain for his friend's return, he grew to hate the places they had been to together, places he had once loved, because they now spoke only of absence and never of possibility. His grief bordered on the despair of someone who had given up wholeness for the fragmentary, momentary delight of living off the restlessness of his pain.

This is how Augustine mourned. He began by asking questions about the nature of his grief. He did not simply feel the sensation of pain and loss, but considered the reason for its intensity. When he asked his soul why it suffered so greatly, he was met with only silence. Next, he applied certain strategies to alleviate the pain. For example, he replaced the sweetness of his friendship with sweet (*dulcis*) tears that delighted his soul. Although there was parity in the replacement—tears instead of friendship—the sense of sweetness and delight was a puzzle he could not resolve to reduce his pain. He wondered whether the sweetness resided in the hope that God might hear his cries. While he thought that such a hope applied to prayers, he was skeptical about whether it applied also to the grief he felt upon losing his friend. Because the tears for his friend asked for nothing and had no hope, they were in no sense a prayer. An expression of *dolor*, they were tears of grief, of mourning, of sorrow.

Augustine considered the possibility that tears, rather than being sweet, were a bitter expression of contempt for the same things that once had been cause for joy. The delight consisted in rejecting the prior delight that now led to pain. Weeping under such circumstances was a bitter delight, because it wallowed in its own resentment.[28] It refused to acknowledge the same prior joy—in this case the friendship—which death had transformed into a source of grief. Acknowledging this perverse delight in the weeping of tears was like saying that he loved his tears more than he had loved his friend. This bitter kind of weeping revealed a deeper truth about the nature of the human condition. It seemed that the bitterness of tears had been an expression of the profound misery he felt, even before he had lost his friend. Death, in that case, had pointed to and aggravated the resentment he felt for his prior existence, bound as it was to the "friendship of mortal things." This was one reason that he both "wept bitterly and was at peace in bitterness."

There was another, implicit, reason that tears, which had once been sweet, grew bitter. It was the recognition that he, as a young man, had put his faith in an imaginary god that could not heal him. There was "peace in bitterness" because "bitterness" brought him closer to unveiling the lie he was living under. On one level, the emotion was consistent with the fact that the Manichaean god he subscribed to offered no tangible relief from his sadness. Because it did not promise the immortality of his friend's soul, there was no hope of ever seeing him again. On another level, death as a Manichaean was a psychological and spiritual enigma that did not conform to the longing and richness of his emotional life. The intensity of his grief was inconsistent with loving a soul that was as imperfect and in need of alteration as the Manichaeans imagined it to be.

Furthermore, the Manichaean experience of salvation was intrinsically unequal, depending on your rank in the sect's hierarchy. The soul of the Elect embarked on a journey of ascent back to the World of Light, a place unlike this earth, where there was no more entanglement with the particles of darkness. It was a place of transcendent disengagement with the flawed reality of this world. In contrast, to die as an auditor—as Augustine and his friend would have died—was to undergo dissolution and transformation along a different, sideways path through the various conditions of spiritual disarray. Jason David BeDuhn has said,

> for the Auditor, there could be no immediate ascent. Instead, the soul was dissolved and "transfused" into disparate states and embodiments, there to continue its odyssey through the cosmos. The individual soul did not cohere, and there was no single state to be imagined for it. Thus, the dead person was

literally gone, and there could be no fantasy of ever meeting him again…Manichaeism did not offer the immortality of the *individual* soul of all believers which was such a hallmark of the appeal of mainstream Christianity.[29]

Without the possibility of the soul continuing as a soul, complete and perfected, there really was no healing for his grief. "Healing" implied "wholeness," and the soul of the Manichaean auditor was intrinsically fragmentary, destined as it was for a journey of alteration through the cosmos. Instead of healing, Augustine experienced a kind of wretched attachment to the misery of his life that he loved, with a perverse delight, even more than he had loved his friend.[30] To say that he had grieved as a Manichaean, though, would be incorrect. He grieved as one for whom the Manichaean teaching had failed and as one who was still a decade away from coming into the flourishing of his Christian self. The *dolor* he felt was a confirmation of his incompleteness.

It left him in a perpetual state of restlessness. The soul he carried with him was tired of being carried, yet he could find no place in which to set it down.[31] In Augustine's words, his soul "did not come to rest in pleasant groves, not in games and songs, nor in sweet smelling places, nor in elaborate banquets, nor in the pleasure of the bed and couch, not, finally, in books and poems."[32] Years later, reflecting on the experience, he knew the reason for his restlessness: the god he had put his hope in at that time was an "empty fantasy and error." Being such a fantasy, this false god produced nothing "steadfast and real" on which to release the burden of his pain. And so it traveled with him wherever he went. "To where," he asked, "could my heart flee from my heart? To where, indeed, could I flee from me myself? To where would I not follow myself?" The challenge for Augustine was that grief had become linked with the physicality of place and lodged in a soul that he did not comprehend.

The philosopher Alice Koller has captured brilliantly the sensation of being overrun by an unrelenting grief that inhabits every aspect of every thing that you are:

What is it to mourn? It is to be hurled into pain so vast that you cannot imagine it in advance of being incorporated by it, a pain that usurps all other thinking, all other feeling, a pain that occupies you as you occupy the house you live in. While the pain that is mourning appropriates you, making you identical with it, so that you do nothing but only mourn, you will cry out, "How have all the millions of people before me endured this?"[33]

"A pain that occupies you as you occupy the house you live in" is a pain that moves in, unpacks its memories, and doesn't leave until you kick it out. Augustine tried to release his pain by vacating his house and moving to Carthage. It was a temporary solution.

From the distance of Carthage he learned that space could be unoccupied, but that time was always full. It rolled through the senses causing "strange operations (*mira opera*)" in the mind, coming and going day by day, introducing "other hopes and other memories."[34] Whereas the emptiness of space had failed to mute his pain, the fullness of time proved a reliable—if superficial—source of healing. "Little by little it restored me with the former kinds of delights, to which this sorrow of mine yielded."[35] The process involved in the healing was more like substitution therapy than it was a genuine, mind-restorative cure. As time "rolled through the senses," new experiences built upon and replaced the earlier times he had loved in the company of his friend. With new friends he made new memories, which consisted in the shared moments of laughing, talking, reading, teaching, and learning that restored him to a fragile steadiness. The problem with such moments was that they were disconnected from the narrative of salvation and its promise of an immortal soul. It left the soul in a fragmented state that depended for its temporary and illusory wholeness upon the comfort of friends, expressed through their demeanor and words. Later, Augustine assessed these times as a "huge fable and a protracted lie," much like the "superstitious and pernicious fables" of Manichaeism that had promised so much and delivered so little.

Perhaps one of the lies he had told himself was that time heals all wounds. By replacing painful memories of loss with new memories of fullness, Augustine had not really mourned at all. The process of momentary substitution had been a superficial pretense that merely dulled his pain. The deep loss he felt prior to acknowledging God was an unrelenting *dolor* that turned "the loss of the life of the dying" into "the death of the living."[36] That was really how he had mourned. In a similar vein, Joan Didion has captured the honest experience of interior desolation: "Nor can we know ahead of the fact (and here lies the heart of the difference between grief as we imagine it and grief as it is) the unending absence that follows, the void, the very opposite of meaning, the relentless succession of moments during which we will confront the experience of meaninglessness itself."[37] Mourning feels the emptiness of time rather than its fullness. It confronts the possibility of the void.

In contrast with the death of his friend, Augustine was conspicuously silent regarding the death of his son, Adeodatus. The silence had nothing to do with any perceived lack of connection or absence of love on his part. Nor did it signal emotional strength or self-control. To the contrary, he had been quite taken with the child, whose talent—in his words—had evoked in him a kind of awe.[38] There is a record of a dialogue between them, *The Teacher*, in which they examine the ways in which language prompts men to learn, while acknowledging that truth, itself, resides only in God.[39] The sixteen-year-old Adeodatus emerges as a worthy interlocutor: he is not led by his father in and out of the various arguments that build inevitably toward the dialectical climax, but contributes to setting the terms. His insights into prayer are a case in point. The words the disciples are taught to pray remind them of the God they are praying to and of what they are praying for. As it takes place in the inner recesses of the mind, prayer is a reminder and a memory of a deep primordial truth that should never be confused with a mundane use of words. As the promising rhetorician that he was, Adeodatus concluded the dialogue with a small rhetorical flourish: "I have learned from the prompting of your words that words do nothing but prompt man to learn." We should take Augustine at his word when he says that the ideas he attributed to his son are an accurate account of what was said. Adeodatus was as impressive as Augustine claimed him to be.

There is a plausible reason for the silence regarding his grief. Because the death of a child violates every law of hope and expectation, there are no words vast enough to capture the emotional anguish. This principle is illustrated by Zadie Smith in a passage of her novel *NW*, where she investigates the shock of looking over the precipice into unimaginable grief:

> She understood that her children were not kidnapped or murdered or likely to be further than 50' from where she was presently standing but running through this logical series of statements did nothing to halt the falling away of everything

that now happened inside her. She peered over into the pit that separates people who have known intolerable pain from people who haven't. Instantly, she was sweating all over her body.[40]

Giving us a glimpse of the terror the mother experienced, Zadie Smith then withdraws that terror to the safety of the imagination. Her words capture the truth of a terrible moment in time and nudge us to generalize from that moment into a series of unthinkable moments that she does not explore further. In maintaining this reserve, Zadie Smith succeeds in capturing the terror of loss where others have failed.

Augustine stepped into that terrifying pit and, thus, separated himself for all eternity from those who have not known intolerable pain.[41] His silence acknowledged this separation, expressing rather the depth of his feeling than the lack of it. As an accomplished literary man and rhetorician, he understood that any attempt to describe his grief risked falling into triteness. Perhaps that is why, at the end of his life, he relied on Cicero to capture the admiration he had felt for his son and, by implication, the magnitude of his loss. Peter Brown has said it best: "In the last book he ever wrote, Augustine will quote a passage from Cicero that, perhaps, betrays the hurt of his loss: 'Surely what Cicero says comes straight from the heart of all fathers, when he wrote: "You are the only man of all men whom I would wish to surpass me in all things."'"[42] While the grief was real, the expression of it would be transformed in the context of spiritual renewal.

Since the last time Augustine had grieved, a decisive change had taken place in how he viewed himself and the world. His emotions were to unfold differently because of it. In this new way of being, it was not possible to nurture a series of unconnected moments and search aimlessly from place to place. He could not recount the loss of his son as he had the loss of his unnamed friend because his grief had evolved according to the new set of priorities required of his renewed commitment to God. It was no longer nourished by the love of self or by the pleasure of emotional introspection for its own sake.

The event that solidified how Augustine would remember his son took place in Milan.[43] Adeodatus accompanied his father and their family friend, Alypius, there that together they might receive the sacrament of baptism from the bishop of Milan, Ambrose.[44] It was

Lent, the designated time to enroll in classes and to undertake the "strict routine of instruction and discipline" in preparation for the rite.[45] As Robin Lane Fox has described it, "Pre-baptismal classes were an arduous business for [Ambrose], as he took them in person, twice a day on at least thirty days in Lent. Candidates heard him in a new context, in a smaller group, intensified by prayer and exhortation."[46]

Although Augustine does not tell us anything about the initiation process, there are two striking features of the narrative, and both are relevant to how he grieved—or how he wants us to think he grieved—for his son. The first is that the death of Adeodatus is connected with baptism; the second is that baptism signals the end of anxiety about the sins they had committed in their former lives. Baptized into Christ, they were now new men ready to "walk in newness of life."[47] In addition to the spiritual transformation, the passage alludes to an emotional transformation that changed how Augustine felt his way through life and, therefore, navigated the emotional traps that had been set for him previously as a Manichaean. While exploring the heresy, he had been impatient for the welfare of his soul. Now he grieved differently because the fear was gone. No longer anxious about his former sins, he likewise "feared nothing about [Adeodatus'] childhood, youth, or about anything at all in him."[48] As Augustine put it, "I remember him freer (*securior*) from care." He chose his word, *securior*, carefully. In the comparative form used here, it implied a greater degree of freedom from care, anxiety, and concern than he had experienced at some prior, undisclosed time. Where we, the readers, are left with virtual silence about the pain of death and about the finer points of baptism, it is worth paying attention to what he does say: Augustine felt mostly untroubled in recalling Adeodatus, because he was confident in his son's virtue and in the atoning power of the sacrament. Their shared baptism into the newness of their Christian life had calmed his fears.

The death of his mother Monica was altogether different from the death of Adeodatus. Whereas silence captured the depth of grief for his son, a kind of wordiness marked his reaction to the death of his mother. Whereas emotions are seemingly held at bay in discussing the loss of his son, they bubble to the surface in recounting the loss of his mother. There are at least two reasons for the differences, the first of which has already been suggested: the death of Adeodatus was simply too painful to expose to our scrutiny and exploit as a rhetorical flourish. Out of this comes the second: we are supposed to perceive the death of Monica in opposition to the death of his friend, not the death of his son. That is why Augustine passes over the death of Adeodatus in relative silence, connecting the episode to the newness of life they received together in baptism, but refusing to lay bare his emotional wounds.

When his friend died Augustine used the word *dolor* to describe his grief. *Dolor* conveyed the feeling of pain in the context of emotional incompleteness. It was as though he had lost half his soul. The pain was so great that he had become a puzzle to himself, not knowing who he was or where precisely he was going. Over time he came to recognize this existential searching as being the real source of his pain. Indeed, he had loved his friend, but the love had been self-serving and inconsequential. In their shared commitment to Manichaeism, he had never learned to love his friend with reference to the eternal love of God.

When his mother died, Augustine used the word *maestitudo* to express the genuine soul-wrenching grief that filled his heart with sadness. Because the feelings were intense and complicated, he also needed the word *tristitia* to express his melancholy sorrow and the word *dolor* to express the painful loss of separation.[49] All three words captured the range of his grief. The most striking feature of the narrative, though, is the tension between the authenticity of his sadness, on the one hand, and the obligation he felt to conceal his sadness by holding back the flow of tears. Apparently a decision had been made by family and friends not to dramatize their feelings with tears, loud cries, and lamentations at the funeral. Such a display was suitable for those who had died in a state of misery and, for that reason, had perished completely. It was inappropriate for someone such as Monica who had died as a Christian with her faith intact. "Neither did she die in a miserable condition, and nor did she die altogether."[50] The passage calls to mind Paul's first letter to the Thessalonians: "We do not want you to be uninformed, brothers and sisters, about those who have died, so that you may not grieve as others do who have no hope" (1 Thess. 4:13). Christian grief was supposed to be different from every other kind of grief. It was tempered by the knowledge of the immortality of the soul and by the hope for the future, bodily resurrection. This new knowledge and hope implied a new way of grieving. Restraint and moderation were to take the place of emotional overindulgence.

Augustine struggled with the limits that this Christian form of grief imposed upon his passions. Although he tried to measure up to the standard of self-control he and others had agreed upon, he noticed that the pain of loss was overwhelming and, therefore, difficult to conceal:

> But in Your ears, where none of them heard, I rebuked the weakness of my feelings and restrained the flow of my grief, which yielded to me somewhat; but its vehemence returned again, not to the point of erupting into tears, nor to changing my expression, though I knew what pressed down upon my heart. And as I was extremely annoyed that these human things had such power over me (which must happen in the due order and destiny of our condition), with another grief I grieved for my grief, and was afflicted by a *double sadness*. (emph. suppl.)[51]

This passage shares with the reader the pain of death, as well as the multidimensional sadness that the Christian feels in its presence. Sadness is the emotional response to loss, it is the object of temperance and moderation in the light of Christian hope, and it reemerges in the context of human failure. The death of Monica is both a test of the controlled expression of grief and proof that grief cannot be controlled altogether while living in the world.

In thinking about a tempered form of grief, Augustine must have considered the Stoics. We have seen how the emotional tranquility of the wise man precluded him from reacting to evil. Insofar as sadness was considered the result of an evil that had already taken place, it was counted among the bad emotions that were morally meaningless—and therefore spiritually impossible—for the Stoic. Yet there was a place for sadness, even among the Stoics. The "double sadness (*duplex tristitia*)" that Augustine referred to in recounting the death of his mother alluded to such a doctrine. This was the Stoics' belief in what they called first- and second-order passions. First-order passions consisted of grief for the loss of an external or bodily good, while second-order passions consisted of grief for the passions that have just been given rise to. With respect to the moral implications of these second-order passions, Johannes Brachtendorf has said, "One can grieve of one's own passions only if one has understood what the real good is, and if one loves it, and knows why passions are an obstacle on the way to the ultimate goal."[52] In alluding to the Stoics, Augustine did not embrace their teaching uncritically. The possibility of feeling a second-order "grief for his grieving" borrowed the best of what the Stoics had to offer, while rejecting the possibility of his achieving emotional tranquility in this lifetime. The appeal of the second-order grief was that it acknowledged the persistence of his emotional response to loss, while rebuking it at the same time. This must have seemed an honest alternative to the Stoic ideal of emotional tranquility. It made it acceptable to grieve as a Christian, as long as you grieved for the spiritual shortcomings of your grief.

A Tradition of Consolation

Augustine would have been aware of the Stoic tradition of letters of consolation and its affirmation of, and challenge to, the stated ideal of emotional equanimity. It was with a kind of Stoic therapy applied to grief that Seneca had comforted his grieving mother, Helvia. Recently, she had lost a grandson and her own son, Seneca, to exile. Like a good physician, he planned to "cauterize and cut" the wound, rather than heal it gently. She was supposed to defeat her pain by confronting it directly, not by sidestepping it into submission.[53] The therapy allied itself to the philosophical assumption that external circumstances are of no significance. Prosperity does not elevate the wise man, nor does adversity bring him down. This was Seneca's unreconstructed Stoic therapy applied to the adverse conditions of real life.

Cicero was more of a Stoic rebel. He had grieved deeply and forthrightly for the death of his beloved daughter, Trullia, who had died a month after giving birth to her second son. There is little attempt at emotional restraint and hardly any shame for failing to uphold some imagined ideal ill-suited to the intensity of his loss. His friend and former student, Servius Sulpicius Rufus, had tried to comfort him in the manner of a Stoic, sharing in his sorrow and then trying to take it away. Cicero resisted. He could think of no eminent person who had lost a child under similar conditions and, therefore, no one to share truly in his pain. The typical Stoic reminder of the transience of all things also failed to console him.

Only a few weeks after his daughter's death Cicero wrote to his close friend, Atticus, "In [my solitude] all conversation is with books. Weeping, nevertheless, interrupts it, which I resist as much as possible, but we are, as of yet, no match."[54] Evident in a letter the next day is a kind of restlessness he does not try to hide, as he longs for the comforting presence of his friend, yet cannot commit himself to any particular place where he might receive it:

> If there were any relief, it would be in you alone, and as soon as it is possible from anyone, it will be from you. Yet at this very time I cannot bear to be without you. But it did not seem right to stay in your house, nor could I stay at mine; and if I were someplace closer, still I would not be with you.[55]

Augustine had expressed a similar agitation when his friend died. There being no place from which to escape his grief, he had found temporary relief in the movement of time and in the unfolding of renewed experience. Although it soothed his pain superficially, this way of mourning did not resolve the spiritual nature of his sadness. The form his grief would take, and the manner in which it unfolded, shifted after his baptism into catholic Christianity. Yet the pain of loss continued to haunt him. When his mother died, for instance, the magnitude of the loss manifested as emotional pain, which produced additional feelings of sadness for his failure to temper his distress. This "second-order" sadness alluded to, and differed from, the sadness of the Stoic wise man, who grieved for his failure to attain the ideal of emotional equanimity. Unlike the grieving Stoic, Augustine regretted his failure to live in the hope of the resurrection and in the expectation of everlasting life. Because the reason for the pain was different, Augustine grieved as a Christian struggling with the manifestation and expression of his emotional turmoil. It was only after the death of his mother and then of his son that he cultivated the feeling of sadness as a virtue. In doing so, he would have to come to terms with the nature and meaning of human suffering in a fallen world, and then articulate what is required of us in the light of Scripture.

Notes

1   Sen., *Ir.*, 3.1.5.
2   Cic., *De or.*, 2.17.72.
3   August., *De civ. D.*, 14.7.
4   Ibid; see also trans. Philip Levine, *Augustine: The City of God.*
    LCL 414 (Cambridge, MA: Harvard University Press, 1966), 293.
5   Ambr., *De vid.*, 6.36; trans. Rev. H. De Romestin, *St. Ambrose.*
    NPNF 10 (Edinburgh: T&T Clark, repr. 1989), 397.
6   August., *Conf.*, 9.12; see trans. Watts, *Confessions*, 57.
7   August., *De ver. rel.*, 12; adapted from trans. John H. S. Burleigh,
    Augustine: Earlier Writings. Library of Christian Classics
    (Philadelphia: The Westminster Press, 1953), 236.
8   See ed. Cornelius Mayer, *Augustinus-Lexicon*, vol. 2 (Basel: Schwabe,
    1996–2002), s.v., 586.
9   August., *De civ. D.*, 14.8.
10 Ibid. 14.7.
11 Ibid. 14.8; see trans. Levine, *The City of God*, 295.
12 Cic., *Tusc.*, 3.1.2.
13 Ibid. 3.2.3.
14 Regarding the public/private distinction, see, for example, Sen.,
    Tranq., 7.3.
15 Ibid. trans. John W. Basore, *Seneca: Moral Essays*. LCL 254
    (Cambridge, MA: Harvard University Press, 1932), 241.
16 Wetzel, "Augustine," 355.
17 James Wetzel, *Augustine and the Limits of Virtue* (Cambridge:
    Cambridge University Press, 1992), 104, discussing Colish, *The Stoic
    Tradition*, vol. 2, 223–4.
18 Robert E. Winn, "Revisiting the Date of Authorship of Basil of
    Caesarea's *Ad Adolescentes*," *The Greek Orthodox Theological
    Review* 44 (1999): 291–307 (303).
19 Cic., *Tusc.*, 4.7.14; see trans. King, *Cicero: Tusculan
    Disputations*, 343.
20 Ambr., *De offic.*, 2.2.4.
21 Mt. 5:11–12.
22 D. A. de Silva, "Ambrose's Use of 4 Maccabees in De Jacob et Vita
    Beata," *Journal of Early Christian Studies* 22, no. 2 (2014): 287–293
    (290); see also ibid. 288.
23 Ambr., *De off.*, 2.5.21; adapted slightly from trans. De Romestin,
    St. Ambrose, 47.
24 Lancel, *St. Augustine*, 41.
25 Ibid. 42.
26 August., *Conf.*, 4.4.

27   Ibid.
28   Ibid. 4.5.
29   BeDuhn, *Augustine's Manichaean Dilemma*, 93.
30   August., *Conf.*, 4.6.
31   August., *Conf.*, 4.7.
32   Ibid.
33   Alice Koller, *Stations of Solitude* (New York: Morrow, 1990), 307.
34   August., *Conf.*, 4.8.
35   Ibid.
36   Ibid. 4.9.
37   Joan Didion, *The Year of Magical Thinking* (New York: A. A. Knopf, 2005), 189.
38   August., *Conf.*, 9.6.
39   That was all Augustine said of the dialogue in his *Retract.*, 1.12.
40   Zadie Smith, *NW* (New York: Penguin Press, 2012), 288–289.
41   A paraphrase of Zadie Smith's words, ibid.
42   Peter Brown, *Augustine of Hippo: A Biography* [first published 1967] (Berkeley: University of California Press, 2000), 128.
43   August., *Conf.*, 9.6.
44   They were baptized on Easter, April 25, 387.
45   Robin Lane Fox, *Augustine: Conversions to Confessions* (New York: Basic Books, 2015), 348.
46   Ibid.
47   My allusion to Rom. 6:4.
48   August., *Conf.*, 9.6.
49   Ibid. 9.12.
50   Ibid; see Watts, *Confessions*, 59.
51   August., *Conf.*, 9.12; see also Watts, *Confessions*, 61.
52   Johannes Brachtendorf, "Cicero and Augustine on the Passions," *Revues des Études Augustiniennes* 43 (1997): 289–308 (295).
53   Sen., *Helv.*, 4.1
54   Cic., *Att.*, 12.15; trans. E. O. Winstedt, *Cicero: Letters to Atticus*, vol. 3 (Cambridge, MA: Harvard University Press, 1961), 31.
55   Cic., *Att.*, 12.16; see trans. Winstedt, *Cicero: Letters to Atticus*, 31–33.

3

Suffering

The sack of Rome in 410 by the Visigothic King Alaric destabilized the conventions of life and worship for rich and poor alike. Members of the aristocracy and others with means who managed to avoid capture fled the city to the relative safety of North Africa. Among them was a monk from Britain, Pelagius, the same man whose ascetic theology of self-imposed moral virtue clashed with Augustine's view of unmerited grace. Pelagius' confidence in the possibility of the individual to rise above the limits of circumstance guided his interpretation of the events unfolding in Rome. Not unlike the monks whose ascetic practice assured them a place in a world that transcended social boundaries and redistributed an unseen grace, the Goths were, in his eyes, the great equalizer. Neither the advantages of wealth nor the certainty of social status could protect the inhabitants of Rome from the ravages of the war-minded Goths.

In practical terms this meant that suffering afflicted nearly everyone the same. The emperor Honorius' twenty-year-old half-sister, Galla Placidia, was taken as a prisoner of war; some Roman citizens were captured and sold into slavery, while others succumbed to famine and disease. Pelagius described the fear and chaos in a world whose social hierarchy had been overturned: "slave and nobility were one; the same image of death was in all, except that those whose life was more pleasant feared its [loss] all the more."[1] Whereas Pelagius emphasized the leveling effects of social disruption, Jerome described the horrors of widespread food shortages:

My voice sticks in my throat; and, as I dictate, sobs interrupt my words. The city that had taken the whole world is seized; in fact, more perished by famine than beforehand with the sword, and scarcely any who were captured have been found. In the heat of frenzy, the people had recourse to unmentionable food and tore each other limb from limb.[2]

Even those who managed to survive the initial sieges, to avoid subsequent captivity, and to find sufficient food were likely traumatized psychologically by the unexpected paradigm shift. Rome had not fallen to a foreign enemy since the sack of the city by the Gauls nearly 800 years earlier. The sense of shock and outrage is captured in Jerome's brief words: "The city that had taken the whole world is seized." He understood that it would no longer be possible to imagine Rome, in the words of Virgil, as the *imperium sine fine*. The eternal city of Rome would have to be reconfigured as a temporal city composed of buildings and monuments, according to new ideological commitments and theological priorities.

Questions from the Pagan Elite

As Augustine began writing *City of God* (*c*.412/3–*c*.426/7), he was thinking about the deeper implications of this shifting political landscape and its consequences for a theology of suffering and of salvation. It is perhaps no accident that the themes he would develop at length, including his criticism of pagan religion and its spurious claims to eternal life, evolved initially in conversation with one of the last pagan hold-outs to conversion.

Rufius Antonius Agrypnius Volusianus was a member of one of the noble, Roman bloodlines, the Caeonii family, whose ancestors had held the prefecture of the city of Rome as a hereditary position since the time of Constantine.[3] A committed pagan, he was among a dwindling class of intelligentsia that persisted in its eloquent expression of pagan values in spite of the pressures closing in on them to the contrary. His family and his life exemplified in microcosm some of the same tensions and divisions that were playing out in Roman society. His father had remained a pagan throughout his life, though his mother and sister were devout Christians, while his niece was the famous desert mother and monastic, Melania the Younger (d. 439).[4] Although Volusianus had been asked to embrace Christianity—probably by his family, but certainly by Augustine—he persevered in his pagan beliefs until the deathbed conversion he experienced with Melania by his side.[5]

Not long after the sack of Rome, Volusianus corresponded with Augustine. Writing from the safety of North Africa, he was among the refugees who had fled the city during the final siege (c.410). In the company of a large group of well-born and educated friends, he found himself discussing the finer points of rhetorical invention, including the beauty of its metaphors, epithets, and illustrations.[6] Suddenly the conversation shifted when one among them related the doubt he was feeling with respect to the truth of the Christian faith. What puzzled him most, we are told, was the paradox of the Incarnation: how could the Lord and ruler of the world have been contained in the womb of a virgin or have undergone the sensations of ordinary men? The conversation that ensued is a window into the mind of a late-Roman pagan trying to navigate the two worlds he now held in tension. His fondness for the rhetorical tropes of pagan poetry, its sublime comparisons, flowing verses, and harmonious spaces, could not have prepared him for the magnitude of the Christian paradox he was facing. The balance, arrangement, and consistency of that literary world were at odds with the precariousness of an Incarnation he could not comprehend.

The generalized sense of anxiety among elite pagans is corroborated in a subsequent letter from Marcellinus, a close friend to Augustine and a high official under the emperor Honorius. In it, Marcellinus confirmed that reservations surrounding the Incarnation persisted among pagans: "The question which he [Volusianus] has submitted to you is indeed worn threadbare in controversy, and the craftiness which, from the same quarter, assails with reproaches the Lord's Incarnation is well known."[7] Apparently it had become commonplace for pagans to assert that the miracles and deeds of their own esteemed magicians, such as Apollonius of Tyana (c.15–c.100) and Apuleius (c.124–c.170), were greater than those of the Lord.

Augustine offered assurances that drew upon the same philosophical principles that Volusianus, Marcellinus, and their circle of friends would have been familiar with. The principles asked them to imagine God's omnipresence in defiance of their limited conceptions of spatial containment. There was a famous passage from Plato's *Timaeus*, for instance, in which a certain invisible and unformed receptacle was understood paradoxically as the substance that received all bodies, without being altered by anything that entered its nature. A metaphorical Mother of the Universe, this was the receptacle of becoming that molded creation, as well as the place in which becoming came into being.[8] Among the early Christians, the biblical scholar and philosophical theologian Origen of Alexandria (d. *c.*253) alluded to this unspecified mode of relating space to matter when he described the omnipresence of God as needing no physical place, magnitude, or body in which to move and exercise being. Like Plato and Origen before him, Augustine similarly evoked the omnipresence of God using the paradoxical language of unconfined space:

> God is not said to fill the world in the same way as water, air, and even light occupy space, so that with a greater or smaller part of Himself He occupies a greater or smaller part of the world. He is able to be everywhere present in the entirety of His being; He cannot be confined in any place; He can come without leaving the place where He was; He can depart without forsaking the place to which He had come.[9]

The paradox of spatial containment shaped Augustine's understanding of God and, by implication, the Incarnation. There was nothing arbitrary or accidental about his allusions to pagan philosophy. It was his way of demonstrating to educated pagans, for whom the Christian faith must have seemed little more than a coarse superstition, the philosophical sophistication of Christianity's claims to truth.

The same group of pagans raised another objection to the faith, which addressed the ideological consequences of the Gothic invasion. They were concerned that the Christian doctrine of love was incompatible with the welfare of the state, specifically with the duties and rights of citizens to retaliate against an enemy or to defend themselves against a foreign invader threatening a Roman province. Biblical passages such as Romans 12:17, "Recompense to no man evil for evil," and Matthew 5:39, "Whosoever shall smite you on one cheek, turn to him the other also," were perceived as obligating passivity in the face of aggression by a foreign invader. Such an ethic was difficult to justify in a time when "very great calamities have befallen the commonwealth under the government

of emperors observing, for the most part, the Christian religion."[10]
To the pagan elite it seemed that the paradox of a suffering savior
who insisted on "turning the other cheek" was out of touch with,
and perhaps even the source of, the series of events that had taken
place recently in Rome.

Augustine developed a series of answers to the problem of
Christian passivity in the context of war that collectively form
what has come to be known as "just war theory." Shortly before
the correspondence with Volusianus, for example, Augustine, in
his *Against Faustus the Manichaean* (*c*.408–410), considered the
possibility that war could be righteous if it were undertaken in
obedience either to a legitimate ruler or to God.[11] There he also
addressed the question Volusianus would later allude to, namely the
apparent contradiction between the Gospel command to "turn the
other cheek and not resist evil" (Mt. 5:39) and God's willingness at
times to enjoin war.[12] In Scripture we are told that the prophets were
commanded to make war, while the apostles were forbidden. For
Augustine, the ostensible incongruity was really just the outward
manifestation of the multidimensional nature of Scripture. Some
passages could be read according to the surface meaning of the text,
while others required a depth of spiritual probing before the correct
interpretation could emerge from the threat of triviality. Such was
the case here in his *Against Faustus*: when Jesus said to "turn the
other cheek and not resist evil" he was talking about a disposition
of the heart and not a bodily action.[13]

I have shown that after the sack of Rome the pagans perceived
a similar tension between the peaceful message of Christ and
the military needs of the state. They feared that Christians were
divided in their loyalty because of it, leaving Rome vulnerable to
its enemies. For Augustine, however, there was no such internal
conflict among Christians. The Roman commonwealth was built, he
said, on a fundamental principle of love, drawn from the scriptural
commandments to love the Lord God with all your heart, soul,
and mind, and to love your neighbor as yourself (Mt. 22:37–39).
He identified three such reasons that this love should govern the
organization of the state. First, God is the cause of everything that
exists, including, one might assume, the political structures that
organize human society. Second, loving God and neighbor in the
manner in which they should be loved results in a good and honest
life. Third, neighbors who love each other for the sake of God

secure the welfare and reputation of the state on a firm foundation of faith.[14] Contrast this way of loving with the man who loves things only as a means to an end that he alone desires, instead of for the particular end that God has appointed.[15] It was only this improper sort of love that threatened the state. Christianity's most fundamental doctrine, its so-called "law of love," was compatible with the law of nations.[16]

Augustine argued further that the Christian doctrine of forgiveness was not at odds with the welfare of the state. We are told that the nobility of pagan Rome had subscribed to a similar teaching that required them to pardon an enemy who had wronged them. He offered the example of Cicero praising the great statesman, Caesar, for having forgotten nothing except for the wrongs his enemies had done to him.[17] Rome had flourished in its affluence and greatness in the light of this moral precept, which served as an ideal to strive for among those operating at the highest levels of the state. For Augustine, the only injustice to consider was that Christians were being criticized for endorsing the same principle of forgiveness that pagans had upheld with much success in the centuries before.[18]

The consistency that Augustine discovered between Christian and pagan ethics implied something specific about the operation of a commonwealth. It functioned best when its interests coincided with the interests of the individual men and women, the *populi*, who made up its citizenry. This is what Augustine meant when he posed the following rhetorical question to Marcellinus: "what indeed is a state (*civitas*), but a multitude of men bound together by a certain bond of concord?"[19] The "bond of concord (*vinculum concordiae*)" was the biblical injunction to "turn the other cheek" and the pagan ethical teaching to do the same. It was also the "concord" that Sallust had spoken of in describing the early formation of the Roman state: "What was a scattered and unsettled multitude [i.e., the Trojans and Aborigines], in a short time, had become by concord a *civitas*."[20] To the extent that Christian doctrine was consistent with ethical principles the pagans had articulated already, Augustine's readers were supposed to conclude that the sack of Rome should not be attributed to Jesus' peaceful message.

Such was the outcome of Augustine's conversation with an elite circle of pagans that included Volusianus and their mutual friend Marcellinus. It was only the beginning of an apologetic discourse about the relationship between Christian teaching and the functioning of the state. It set the stage for a much longer conversation about the meaning of human suffering in the context of history.

Negotiating with Evil

This would take place over the course of the next decade in what Augustine considered his greatest work, *City of God*. Dedicated to the same Marcellinus whom he had been in correspondence with, the book addressed the hypocrisy of pagans who blamed Christians for the sack of Rome, while taking refuge in their churches and martyrs' shrines. The remainder of the book contextualized the current situation in Rome, first, by refuting the pagan view of history and, then, by demonstrating the origins, progress, and destiny of the city of the world, which he contrasted sharply with the eschatological reality of the city of God.[21]

With respect to the world, the pagans had been unrelenting in their criticism of how viciously recent events had unfolded. It seemed to them as if no one was immune, whether pagan or Christian, from the violence the Goths inflicted upon the city. Augustine did not entirely disagree. Everyone had suffered, and he knew it. Where he departed from the pagans was in the eschatological perspective he superimposed upon the moral problem. As he put it, "A dissimilarity remains among those who suffer even when there is a similarity of suffering, and although the suffering takes place by means of the same torment, virtue and vice are not the same."[22]

How precisely were they different, and why did it matter? Those who lived their lives according to the principles of the Christian faith were, he said, nothing like the pagans. This was not because Christians were morally superior. Drawn in by the world's enticements, Christians sometimes faltered along their path. Yet, as we shall see in Chapter 6, Augustine knew that Christians were made righteous, first, by their faith and then, secondarily, by the works they performed in the context of faith. Christian virtue was the outward manifestation of the inner transformation that happened through faith and by the divine operation of grace. To the extent that Christians lived out the imperative of their faith, they constituted the true body of Christ. In contrast with pagans whose lack of faith in God brought them to condemnation, Christians looked forward to eternal life in the world to come. The apparent similarity in suffering between these two groups did not alter this fundamental difference in eschatological orientation.

The question as to why Christians and pagans suffered alike in this world remained. For Augustine, it had nothing to do with either the unresponsiveness of the Christian faith or its indifference toward virtue and vice. It was rather a problem of moral discernment on the part of Christians who loved their present life and made their ethical decisions accordingly.[23] They saw the sins of those in power, but were afraid to expose them to scrutiny, for fear that, in doing so, they might compromise their personal safety, reputation, and fortune. Their nonintervention was, in the words of Augustine, "due to certain bonds of selfishness, not the duties of love."[24] It was a question of choosing their continued enjoyment of the things of this world over the disruption that might occur if they were to confront the evil around them. In failing to call this evil out, Christians perpetuated and implicitly consented to the system. Their complacency led them to suffer nearly the same punishments in history as their pagan counterparts. The apparently similar punishment betrayed their similar love for, and benefit from, the pleasures and security that this world had to bring. This misplaced love justified the torment that Christians and pagans endured in the course of political events.

Although Christians and pagans loved the world similarly, Augustine suggested they did so to varying degrees. Pagans were committed to the pleasures of this world as an end in itself, while Christians, in accommodation to the social and political incentives developed by the pagans, had become habituated to worldly advantages. The pursuit of Christian virtue in such a fallen world was flawed and difficult, though, for the reasons suggested, not fatally so. There was, in other words, a continuum of love among Christians that was influenced by the city of man, rather than the singular commitment to loving the city of God that Augustine called for. This continuum of love for temporal things explained why Christians were slightly better situated than pagans with respect to the world and its priorities. Unlike the pagans, they had adapted to the world more than they had loved it. Still, this process of adaptation along a continuum of love accounted for the presence of suffering among Christians.

The connection Augustine drew between the ethical inadequacy of a citizenry and its state-induced suffering was different from what we find among classical Latin authors and the Christian theologies of history that followed. Sallust, for instance, attributed the success of the early inhabitants of Rome to the overall thriving of its population, its arable land, and its moral conduct.[25] There were certainly practical reasons that well-behaved Roman tribes would share in political success.

Such Christian authors as Orosius (d. *c*.418), a student of Augustine, nuanced this correlation between morals, on the one hand, and rewards and punishments, on the other, by developing a theology of history that correlated political change with the progress of the faith. The advent of Christ, he argued, was providentially coincident with the *pax romana* of the first Roman emperor, Caesar Augustus.[26] Like Eusebius of Caesarea (d. *c*.339/340) before him, he viewed this unprecedented peace as ushering in the beginning and subsequent spread of the Christian faith. Time being divinely guided, he envisioned a threefold division of history that consisted in the beginning of the world until the founding of Rome; the history of Rome until the end of the Republic; and the age of Augustus and the birth of Christ until the present day, the third and final period that was supposed to bring about salvation.[27]

Shortly after Carthage fell to the Vandals in 439, another Christian historian, Salvian of Marseilles, adopted a similar view of history as divinely guided. The moral logic with which he interpreted political events led him to praise the invading barbarians for their virtue and to condemn the Christians morally for their military failure: "I shall, with divine assistance, prove clearly," he said, "that God's favor was as just to the Romans in the past as God's severity is just toward us currently, and that the help by which God exalted the Romans was as deserved then as we deserve to be punished now."[28] He defended the underlying justice of divine providence to the point of ascribing virtue to the barbarians and moral breakdown to the Christians.

For Augustine, there was no such providential ordering of human affairs, because history consisted in a series of discrete, monumental occurrences that had little or nothing to do with divine intervention. Such watershed events as the sack of Rome reflected the worldly commitments of human beings and their selfish preoccupations, not the eternal commitments of the city of God. Unlike the utopian republic described by Plato, which Augustine would have known in Latin translation, there was no ideal commonwealth where suffering was held at bay. The Christians continued to suffer in the context of history for the reasons suggested. They had benefited materially and socially from a political system they knew was corrupt, but refused to expose. Their love for the city of man, and the benefits they reaped from it, offered a comfort they could not let go of.

Defeat of Pagan Philosophy

Stoic philosophy addressed the problem of such misdirected love by examining what precisely the wise man should deem relevant to his moral flourishing. It concluded that the pleasures of honor, reputation, and wealth were fleeting and, therefore, nonessential to the acquisition and maintenance of the deeper and more lasting virtue of the wise man. By keeping his priorities straight, the wise man maintained emotional equanimity. In times of collective trauma, he learned to separate himself from the vicissitudes of history. If a Stoic were asked why the morally good suffered, he might have replied that it simply cannot be so. Due to his commitment to his own moral virtue, the wise man did not fall prey to the same emotional traps as the typical Roman citizen. He knew what did and did not matter and adjusted his emotional responses accordingly.

Augustine examined this system of cognitive modification in the context of the challenges pertaining to the city of man and the theological commitments of the Christian faith. The discussion emerged from his larger rhetorical preoccupations with respect to the presence of suffering among Christians and pagans alike in times of political transformation. I have shown that he, as well as others, perceived that individual Christians who pursued a life of virtue in the context of faith suffered the same misfortunes of history as their so-called faithless pagan counterparts. This unsettling observation contradicted the findings of such providential historians as Orosius and, later, Salvian of Marseilles, both of whom attributed the suffering they witnessed to the moral failure of the citizenry. In such a moral universe, there would have been no discernible reason to elevate grief and compassion—emotions pagan philosophy had rejected—to the status of a virtue. Suffering that was deserved did not merit a compassionate response.

Augustine developed a more nuanced view. That suffering could be explained and justified did not necessarily mean it was deserved. This was the reason he set out to defeat pagan philosophy on its own terms: he wished to account for the fact that Christians and pagans suffered together *and* that the justice of God continued to operate in the world. Such a tension between reality and truth did not arise among pagans, for whom there was no unjust suffering. There was only the suffering that followed from an incorrect cognitive response to the unfortunate events of their lives. The wise men whom the pagans admired were distinguished by their ability to prioritize their emotional equanimity over the outward demonstration of their pain. They understood that the only thing worth caring about was the attainment of personal virtue. In such a moral universe, compassion for other people's suffering would have been unnecessary.

Augustine resolved the problem of unjust suffering and undercut the pagans by constructing a rhetorical argument. His method should not be viewed as a dismissal of all such pagan philosophical claims to truth. We shall bear this in mind while tracing the development of a Christian moral psychology that responded to the needs of Christians suffering in the context of political upheaval. Augustine's confrontation with pagan moral psychology began with a summary of a philosophical disagreement. We are told in *City of God*, book 9, that philosophers differ as to whether the wise man experienced certain "emotions of the rational soul" (*motus animi*), the so-called "perturbations," "passions," and "affections" of pagan moral thought. He goes on to say that even if it could be shown that the wise man experienced such emotions, the philosophers could not articulate the degree to which, and the conditions under which, he did so.[29] Augustine was referring to the debate between the Stoic and Aristotelian Peripatetic philosophers that Cicero had described in the *Tusculan Disputations*.[30]

For Cicero, the ideal Stoic wise man was the model of emotional equanimity. He was tranquil and, therefore, happy, because he understood the relative insignificance of human affairs in the light of the vastness of the universe and then trained his mind according to its "right reason (*recta ratio*)." Quieted by the practice of moderation and consistency, "he is neither consumed with distress, nor shaken with fear, nor does he burn with desire for something he eagerly seeks, nor pine away longingly with a futile eagerness."[31] In contrast with the Stoics, we are told that the Aristotelian Peripatetics believed that the rational soul (animus), including the soul of the wise man, experienced a degree of emotional disturbance limited only by the virtuous exercise of his will. No amount of cognitive training could remove such emotions entirely, first, because they were natural and, second, because they served certain useful ends. Anger, for instance, correlated with righteous indignation, fear correlated with caution, and desire with motivation. What Cicero found objectionable was not the presence of emotion per se—the Stoics, after all, permitted good emotions—but the willingness to let the slippery slope of emotional vices into the wise man's experience. There was no reason to risk emotional degradation in the light of the fact that "all emotional disturbances are in our power, all submit to judgment, and all are voluntary."[32]

The dispute, as Cicero saw it, was between the cognitive model of moral psychology favored by the Stoics and the precognitive model of the Peripatetics, each of which had consequences for how the wise man perceived his emotions and undertook to moderate them. At stake was the relative value of self-control with respect to human flourishing in the context of a just and ordered Roman society. The same "right reason" governing the universe was the measure by which the wise man judged his emotional restraint.

For Augustine, the moral priorities were different. Society was not the efficient model of justice mirrored on the all-pervasive god of nature.[33] He understood the fatalism of a Stoic pantheistic naturalism that made god the "world itself" (ipse mundus), the "common nature of things" (communis rerum natura), the "fated force" (fatalis vis), and the "necessity of future events" (necessitas rerum futurarem).[34] It might seem counterintuitive that a philosophy steeped in fatalism believed that human beings determined the value they attached to material goods, experiences, and emotions. Such fatalism should have been opposed to the possibility of self-determination. Yet Augustine saw that, for the Stoics, it was consistent with the internal submission of their wise man to external events over which he believed he had no control and to which he attached nothing of value.

Augustine rejected both psychological models, the natural emotions of the Peripatetics and the cognitive emotions of the

Stoics. Instead of underscoring their differences, however, he made them substantially agree. It was a sharp rhetorical maneuver that subordinated pagan philosophy to the demands of the time and to the development of a distinctly Christian moral psychology. As James Wetzel has observed, Augustine's "reinterpretation of Stoicism to have it join Peripatetic psychology is far from innocuous, for in depriving pagan psychology of Stoicism's radical ambition to free us wholly from inner turmoil, Augustine in effect describes philosophy's fall from grace."[35] Augustine built his reevaluation of pagan philosophy on a clever reading of Cicero, whose book *On Ends* considered whether Aristotle, Plato, and the Stoics were largely in agreement as to the content and value of virtue for the wise man's moral progress.[36] The debate focused on determining the validity of certain terminological distinctions the Stoics had made with respect to external things they deemed beneficial that were other than the ultimate good. For the Stoics, the term "good" was supposed to be used only to describe the virtue of the rational soul, while the term "advantages" was used to describe every type of external thing the wise man might value inappropriately, including the advantages of health, reputation, and wealth. The Aristotelians, in contrast, valued something they called "external goods" and, therefore, did not make virtue the only possible good the wise man attained.

Augustine combined two related arguments from Cicero's *On Ends* to strike one devastating blow against pagan moral psychology. There really was no difference, he said, between the Stoics and Aristotelians, both of whom ascribed some sort of value to external things. He was drawing, first, upon Cicero's interlocutor, Antiochus, who represented the philosophical commitments of the Old Academy, which sought to combine Platonism, Aristotelianism, and Stoicism into a single tradition; and, second, upon Cicero's criticism that Stoicism offered nothing in this regard that was philosophically new. As Augustine put it, "The result is that, no matter what they are called by either of the two, whether 'goods' or 'advantages,' they are, nonetheless, judged by an equal estimation, and on this question, the Stoics merely delight in the novelty of words."[37] For Cicero, the coherence of Stoicism as a philosophical system was at stake. For Augustine, it was the relationship between pagan and Christian moral thought: were the two systems incompatible, or were they fundamentally the same?

Such questions formed the lens through which Augustine assessed the wise man's experience of certain mental passions (*passiones animi*). Significant in this regard is the *Attic Nights* of Aulus Gellius (d. *c.*180s), a compilation of conversations he had heard and notes he had taken on such varied topics as philosophy, history, geometry, and philology. Most relevant for Augustine's purpose of constructing a moral psychology was the record of a conversation Gellius had overheard while aboard a ship sailing the Ionian Sea during a violent storm. An eminent Stoic philosopher whom he had known at Athens was also aboard the ship. Gellius decided to locate him to learn whether he was terrified by the looming threat or whether he remained undaunted. What he found was something in between. The Stoic was not crying out or weeping, as some of the others were doing, yet he was trembling and pale, so that "in the disturbance of his color and expression he was not that different from everyone else."[38] When the sea grew calm again, a wealthy Greek man from Asia Minor approached the Stoic, taunting him thus: "What is this all about, philosopher, that when we were in danger, you were afraid and turned pale, while I was not afraid and did not turn pale?"[39] Offended by the question, the Stoic replied tersely that he, being virtuous, had more to lose than the Greek man, and, therefore, more to fear. Later that evening, Gellius approached the Stoic to learn the true reason for his expression of fear.

The Stoic referred him to the Greek philosopher Epictetus (d. 135), whose *Discourses*, book 5 (no longer extant) outlined the conditions under which the wise man experienced certain terrifying mental visions (*visa animi*, in the Latin, or *phantasiai*, in the Greek).[40] For Epictetus, the rational faculty was supposed to evaluate such mental visions or "appearances" with respect to an overarching moral framework that made the best use of things within our power, while using the rest according to their nature.[41] Consistent with the Stoic theory of perception, those first appearances of an object were thought to exert a certain power of their own that had to be perceived.[42] While this preliminary perception was assumed to be involuntary, the wise man's assent to it was subject to his will. In practical terms, this meant that the mind (*animus*) of the wise man might, "from certain swift and unexpected movements that outpace the function of the mind (*mens*) and of reason (*ratio*),"[43] feel disturbed for a little while. The wise man did not approve of, consent to, or confirm such mental visions, but rather cast them aside and rejected them. Because the fool, in contrast, believed that these appearances were just as terrifying as they seemed to be when they initially impacted his mind, he consented to them as if they were real. The difference was that the wise man, even as he trembled, retained the steady judgment (*sententia*) that such mental visions incited merely the false appearance of dread.

The story Augustine related about the trembling wise man was really about the defeat of pagan moral psychology on its own terms. First, it demonstrated that the Stoics were not all that different from the Peripatetics in ascribing to the wise man the mind (*mens*) and reason (*ratio*) needed to overcome the passions and disturbances that, from time to time, afflict the rational soul (*animus*). Essentially the argument rejected Epictetus' so-called "mental visions," those incipient experiences of fear that outpaced the rational capacity of the *mens* to control them. For Augustine, what the Stoics called "involuntary perceptions" were just the "advantages" and "disadvantages" they had spoken of. They were the same things the philosopher judged worthy, or not, for his flourishing. This meant that the incipient sensation of fear the Stoic philosopher felt while aboard the imperiled ship was the consequence of the fundamental judgment that he valued the life he was in danger of losing. For Augustine, this positive assessment of life and limb in the context of the wise man's experience should not be considered a rejection of his preliminary passions, but rather as a reinterpretation.[44] "Nevertheless, he was truly able both to endure that emotion and to hold firmly by the judgment that this life and bodily welfare, the loss of which was threatened by the savage storm, are not goods that make those to whom they belong good, as does righteousness."[45]

This takes us to Augustine's second point in defense of a unified moral psychology. No matter which philosophical school applied, the Stoic or the Peripatetic, the wise man valued righteousness over every other good. Inasmuch as this overarching principle governed the wise man's mind (*mens*), no perturbations of his rational soul (*animus*) could prevail against it. Even while trembling in fear, the wise man kept a measure of control over his passions that kept him consistently wise. A brief quotation from Virgil summarized the matter for Augustine: "His mind (*mens*) remains unmoved, tears flow in vain."[46]

A third point follows from the prior two to reveal why Augustine constructed a cohesive pagan philosophy, in which

Stoics, Platonists, and Peripatetics are made to agree. Such an alliance served as the intellectual foundation for a Christian moral psychology that was just as venerable as the paganism that had attempted to defeat it. The alliance addressed the concerns of Volusianus and his circle of pagan elites, by demonstrating that the biblical message of peace and compassion had not undermined the security of the state. These ideals were consistent with the pagan philosophical principles Augustine had found buried amid their endless disagreements. When exposed to scrutiny, the wise men of the Stoics were revealed to be nearly as interested in their emotional life as the Christians, whose values derived from Scripture. Consistent with the philosophical past, Christianity and its ethical commitments were not responsible for the sack of Rome and the suffering of its citizenry.

A Christian Moral Psychology

In the light of Augustine's rebuke of pagan philosophy, it might seem surprising that he made his moral psychology harmonious with their fundamental beliefs. Yet that is precisely what happened when he folded the ethical demands of Scripture into the philosophical equation: "Scripture subjects the mind (*mens*) itself to God, that it be ruled and supported, and [subjects] the passions to the mind (*mens*), that they be moderated and restrained, and then transformed for the service of righteousness (*iustitia*)."[47] Recall that the same principle of righteousness governed the *mens* of the wise man, thereby preventing certain unruly passions from overcoming his *animus*. For Christians and pagans alike, the *mens* was supposed to conform to righteousness in order to control the manner in which the emotional life unfolded. The underlying context and mechanism for emotional integrity was the same.

Christian moral psychology distinguished itself from the pagans in its commitment to the scriptural norms that gave new ethical content to the meaning of "righteousness" (*iustitia*). For Augustine, righteousness that is grounded in Scripture keeps the emotions of the *animus* in check. Yet, the process of emotional control is not without its challenges. Similar to the pagan wise man, the *animus* of the Christian must deal with the initial emotions of anger and sadness. The moral resolve of the wise man often requires him not to consent to such fledgling emotions. The Christian, in contrast, aligns such emotions felt by the *animus* with the higher purpose of a *mens* that is governed by, and aligned with, the righteousness of God. Augustine, thus, distinguished the lower feeling of "anger" from the righteous feeling of "moral outrage," the morally ambiguous feeling of "sadness" from the ethical feeling of "pity" or "compassion," and the cowardice of "fear" from courageous intervention on behalf of another human being.

To be fair, the Stoics also recognized a subset of good emotions (*eupatheiai*) that were permitted, and even encouraged, for the wise man to feel. These included the feeling of "joy," such as "delight," "mirth," and "cheerfulness," the feeling of "caution," such as "modesty" and "reverence," and the feeling of "well-reasoned desire," which included "benevolence," "friendliness," "respect," and "affection."[48] Given these possibilities for emotional flourishing, it would be misleading to describe the Stoic wise man as having achieved passionlessness, a theoretical state that they themselves rejected for its apparent ruthlessness. Both Stoic and Christian moral psychology allowed for some manner of emotional engagement.

Augustine differed from the Stoics in giving particular weight to compassion (*misericordia*) as a good emotion that Christians should nurture. Seneca, for example, had distinguished "pity," which he found acceptable and even desirable as a virtue worth pursuing, from "compassion," which he criticized as a sign of emotional weakness.[49] He objected to the indignity of emotional contagion. Even Cicero, whom Augustine praised for acknowledging compassion as a virtue, had elsewhere mentioned it among the undesirable perturbations that the wise man should restrain.[50] Cicero also compared it to the vice of envy, in the sense that both compassion and envy involved the inappropriate feeling of pain over the circumstances of another human being.[51] The philosopher was supposed to maintain his emotional boundaries.

The preservation of such boundaries at any cost was precisely what Augustine had found unacceptable. As Sarah Catherine Byers has shown, the sort of compassion Augustine had in mind was the feeling of pity that the virtuous person cultivated with respect to the moral and physical welfare of another human being.[52] The trembling wise man that Gellius told of was problematic for Augustine because he had been more concerned for his personal safety than he had been for the moral virtue of a fellow human being.[53] It was the difference between self-centered fear as a fledgling emotional state that happened in the *animus*, and other-regarding compassion (*misericordia*) as an affective response to human suffering. As Augustine put it, "What is compassion (*misericordia*) but a kind of sympathy (*compassio*) in our heart for the suffering (*miseria*) of another that surely compels us to help as much as we can?"[54] In other words, *misericordia* is a sympathy felt in the heart, for the suffering of another human being, that inspires some kind of compassionate response. It is not "pity" in the pejorative sense of the word. It does not condescend to human suffering, as if it were remote from possibility. Instead, it accepts the experience of another as so relevant to our own well-being that we must act in order to alleviate the condition of suffering. This is the kind of suffering that we not only perceive in another but that we ourselves feel on behalf of another and for ourselves through another, because we sense that it is inevitable.

Christ's death on the cross, which Christ underwent to redeem our spiritual wounds, had changed the meaning of suffering. It was no longer simply an existential condition that asked to be tolerated, as it had been among the pagans. Now it had a moral and therapeutic significance that rendered those who endured its pain into the embodiment of redemptive virtue, as I shall discuss further in Chapter 6. There is a spiritual triumph in shared suffering that is captured in the old English poem *The Dream of the Rood* (*c.* 8th century).[55] The cross, as witness to the transformative power of Christ's suffering, is made to speak of the anguish it shared: "They skewered me with dark nails, wounds easily seen upon me,/Treacherous strokes yawning open. I dared injure none of them./They shamed us both together. I was besplattered with blood,/sluicing out from the man's side, after launching forth his soul./Many vicious deeds have I endured on that hill—/I saw the God of Hosts racked in agony./Darkness had covered over with clouds/the corpse of the Sovereign, shadows oppressed/the brightest splendor, black under breakers./All of creation wept, mourning the king's fall—/Christ was upon the cross" (lines 46–56). It was not only Christ who suffered on the cross but the cross that suffered with him, and in and through its suffering witnessed all of creation mourning the injustice of his pain. In the midst of this shared suffering, the wood of the cross was transformed from being an apparatus used for torture to an instrument of redemption: "On me the Child of God suffered awhile. Therefore I triumphant/now tower under the heavens, able to heal/any one of them, those who stand in terror of me" (lines 83–86). As both the cause of suffering and the means of it being overcome, the cross becomes our triumph over unjust suffering.

The universal suffering of Christ on the cross provides Christians with so much more than an example of moral conduct to be followed and imitated. Indeed, for Augustine, emulating the virtue that Christ lived on earth and died for on the cross does not necessarily suffice to make us morally good. The motivation for moral conduct must extend beyond the anticipation of individual achievement. Potentially discounting the plight of the other, such actions are often self-involved and, for that reason, inconsistent with the obligation to care deeply and sincerely for those who are suffering. The obligation includes those "impulses and emotions that come from love of the good and of holy charity" and thus requires a level of emotional engagement that challenges the pagan commitment to personal virtue as an end in itself.[56]

Christ exemplified this paradigmatic shift to perfection. During his earthly ministry, Christ displayed such emotions as sorrow and anger to align himself with our human emotions and, in that way, heal our suffering, as we shall see in Chapter 5. In contrast with human beings who often lose control of themselves in times of grief, Christ felt the emotions he felt willingly, because he, as the redeemer, experienced the fullness of the human condition. Affectivity in Christ was, therefore, never a sign of weakness, but of the paradoxical expression of his power to heal.

When Augustine deprived pagan moral psychology of its philosophical differences he reconfigured the intellectual justification for our affective engagement with human suffering. The artificial distinction the pagans had drawn between "external goods," on the one hand, and "advantages," on the other, proved to Augustine that they preferred disputation to truth and words to reality.[57] In constructing a unified moral psychology that could be applied universally, he had rendered their philosophical distinctions meaningless. It elevated the emotions of the wise man to the category of "goods" that were relevant to the wise man's flourishing and a legitimate object of his moral concern.

Augustine applied the same standard to Christians, who believed similarly that certain emotions were morally good and, therefore, relevant to the progress of virtue. The difference from the pagans resided in the content of the truth claims that shaped this new moral world. Christians, who did not "prefer contention to the truth and words to reality," applied their own criterion for virtue. It was the "sound doctrine" of their Scriptures and the rightness of their love that had taught them to feel "fear and desire, grief and gladness while they live according to God in the sojourning of this life."[58] These same feelings Christians feel for themselves they are supposed to feel for others whom, as Augustine put it, "they desire to be set free and fear might perish, whom they grieve if they perish and rejoice if they are set free."[59]

In this moral framework, emotional tranquility as an ideal was called into question. Among the Stoics, for whom "divine power resided in reason and in the mind and intellect of universal nature,"[60] the "right reason" that governed the universe also served as the standard for their moral reasoning. The world the Stoics imagined was just, ordered, and true had the principle of its destruction in the conflagration, which was also the source of past, present, and future events.[61] Because everything in their world unfolded according to "an inescapable law of what exists," the mind was capable of being restrained and disciplined in correspondence with its orderly arrangement.

After the sack of Rome the world had changed. Suffering could no longer be accounted for by imagining the individual in Stoic terms, as just one more link on the chain of cosmic reason. Nor could it be accounted for by connecting the extent of one's suffering with the quality of one's virtue. Good people did indeed suffer, and not all suffering was morally deserved. (How different this was from the political theologies of Orosius and Salvian of Marseilles.) This new world was a place where Christians suffered in the context of history, for the corruption of others, and for their complacency in failing to disclose it.

For Augustine, a moral universe in which Christians continued to suffer demanded a new mode of emotional engagement. Whereas the emotions of Christ were felt only when he decided to feel them,[62] human beings feel their emotions even when they try to repress them. In the light of this truth, emotional conviction is not a weakness, but rather a vital concession to the reality of the present life: "Although at times we are moved not by guilty desire, but by praiseworthy charity, we weep even when we do not wish to... But if we were to have no such feelings at all while bearing the weakness of this life, then rather would we not be living rightly."[63] The evils of this world were challenging enough that no amount of emotional discipline could stop the Christian from feeling other people's suffering. Nor should it. The only self-imposed restraint was the direction of one's emotional aspirations, so that "a right sort of life has all these emotions in a right way, and a bad life, in a bad way."[64]

Angels were different. Augustine thought they were capable of punishing without anger, of ministering to those who were suffering without themselves undergoing suffering, and of assisting loved ones in danger without feeling fear.[65] Their emotions were modeled on ours because of a generic likeness to certain of our behaviors. Demons were likewise in a category of their own. Tossed about by the irrational impulses of their mind, they were the subject of emotional fluctuation. Whereas human beings experience impulses in the *animus*, we are told that demons experience them in the mind (*mens*), the place where such passions would come under control ordinarily. In making this distinction, Augustine equated the mind of the demon, which is a slave to passion and devoid of wisdom, to that of the fool who has no truth. Among virtuous Christians who are nothing like fools, affectivity is a provisional concession to this life of suffering. To the extent that emotional engagement with human suffering is necessary to live a virtuous life here in the city of man, it is then dispensed with in the city of God. This elevated state is distinct from the demons, but not all that different from that of the angels, for whom no felt emotions are needed to act compassionately.

Augustine explored the relationship between human and angelic suffering in his exposition of Psalm 42. In it, he compared the act of praising God on the lyre with the similar act of praising God on the psaltery. Both instruments were good when the musician playing them was trained adequately. They differed mainly in the orientation of the sound box from which the music emanated, the psaltery being played with the sound box facing upward, and the lyre with it facing downward.[66] For Augustine, this distinction between the higher (*superior*) and lower (*inferior*) sound box signified the orientation of our works and the possibility of our suffering in the world.[67] Much like the angels, he said we "play the psaltery" and trigger our higher orientation when we follow God's commands and consequently do not suffer. We "play the lyre" from our lower orientation when we suffer tribulation, the scandals of this world, and the things done to us by those not "from above."

Augustine's recommendation was twofold: we should either play the ten-stringed psaltery by obeying God's ten commandments, or play the lyre by patiently enduring suffering.[68] Both options were morally acceptable. The ability to play either one competently was necessary for a life lived in the context of an imperfect world filled with "sorrow, sickness, trials, troubles, and temptation."[69] With respect to the downward orientation of the lyre, he noted that personal anguish could become morally beneficial if it were converted to alleviate someone else's suffering. For instance, the food given up in fasting could be used profitably to feed another human being.

"To play the lyre" was not just a strategy for managing the trials of this world. It was a call to action in the light of human suffering that was not without its challenges. Augustine acknowledged, for instance, that sometimes people felt grief-stricken in their compassion at the sight of other people's misery.[70] Those inclined to suffer such emotional pain were urged to recall that in the world to come there will be no need to alleviate sorrow. Until that time, the possibility of experiencing shared grief was never supposed to prevent someone from undertaking the duty of compassionate care. In his early years, Augustine had warned about the risk of what we might call "compassion fatigue." We are to confront the misery of another human being without ourselves becoming incapacitated by it.[71] He suspected that the wise man had rejected compassion as a moral ideal so as to avoid the unwanted feeling of emotional pain.[72] In contrast with the emotionally guarded wise man, Christians are supposed to feel compassion while alleviating their emotional distress in the context of the steady love of God.[73]

Christ is the archetype of compassionate care. He felt the pain of human misery to heal fallen humanity of its sins. The emotional component of Christ's ministry on earth is deeply connected to the purpose of the Incarnation:

> Hear the apostle wishing to commend [Christ's] compassion (*misericordia*) to us, because for our sake he was made weak that he might gather chicks under his wings (Matt 23:37), as he taught the rest of the disciples, that they themselves might

feel compassion (*compatior*) for the weakness of the weak, those who had ascended to a certain strength from a common weakness; when this one descended from the celestial strength to our weakness, the Apostle says to them, "Feel this in you, which is also in Christ Jesus." "See fit," he says, "to imitate the Son of God through sympathy (*compassio*) with the little ones."[74]

Just as Christ "emptied himself in the form of a slave" that he might become weak for our sake, we, in imitation of the weakness he assumed voluntarily, are meant to feel compassion for the weakness of those who are suffering. Our feelings in the context of suffering are modeled on the emotional state of Christ during his ministry. Nothing could be further from the ideal of the wise man seeking to maintain his emotional tranquility in the light of human misery. For Christians, the highest ideal is to feel the same compassion Christ felt for the weakest of the weak and to imitate the divine compassion.

Feeling compassion for the suffering of another is necessary in this fallen world to which Christians have surrendered. Augustine's moral psychology, which ascribed virtue to human emotion in the context of suffering, did not undermine the welfare of Rome, as certain elite pagans feared. It elevated the ethical and spiritual life of the Christian above the indifferent abstraction of the pagan state, where the individual was measured in terms of his conformity to an illusory standard. Augustine replaced this illusion with the truth he found in the unfolding of our emotional life. By realigning human emotion according to the principles of Scripture, he articulated how Christians were to respond to, and make sense of, the apparently unjust suffering that occurred among Christians and pagans alike when the Visigoths sacked Rome. And by realigning these emotions and experiences with the Incarnation, he unlocked the method of our salvation.

Notes

1   Pelag., *Ep. ad Dem.*, 30 (413); see trans. B. R. Rees, *The Letters of Pelagius and His Followers* (Woodbridge: Boydell Press, 1991).

2   Jer., *Ep.*, 127.12 (412).

3   Lancel, *St. Augustine*, 314.
4   Ibid.
5   Geront., *Vit. S. Melan.*, 53–5.
6   August., *Ep.*, 135.
7   Ibid. 136.1; trans. J. G. Cunningham, *Letters of St. Augustine.* NPNF 1 (Edinburgh, T&T Clark, repr. 1994), 472.
8   Pl., *Ti.*, 51A, ed. I. Burnet, *Platonis Opera* (Oxford, 1984); ibid. 50C/D; ibid. 49B.
9   August., *Ep.*, 137.4; trans. Cunningham, *Letters of St. Augustine*, 474.
10 Ibid. 136.2; trans. Cunningham, *Letters of St. Augustine*, 473.
11 August., *C. Faust. Man.*, 22.75.
12 Ibid. 22.76.
13 Ibid.
14 August., *Ep.*, 137.17.
15 August., *C. Faust. Man.*, 22.78.
16 For the phrase "law of love," see August., *De doct. Christ.*, 1.22.21.
17 August., *Ep.*, 138.9.
18 Ibid. 138.10.
19 Ibid.; trans. Cunningham, *Letters of St. Augustine*, 484.
20 Sall., *Cat.*, 6.2., cited by Augustine, *Ep.*, 138.10; trans. Cunningham, *Letters of St. Augustine*, 484.
21 As described by August., *Retract.*, 2.69.
22 August., *De civ. D.*, 1.8.
23 Ibid. 1.9.
24 Ibid.; adapted from trans. George E. McCracken, *Saint Augustine: The City of God against the Pagans*. LCL 411 (Cambridge, MA: Harvard University Press, repr. 1995).
25 Sall., *Cat.*, 6.2.
26 See Oros., *Hist. adv. pag. l vii*, 1.2, 3.8, 6.17, 6.20, 6.22, 7.2. Orosius thought that the empire of Caesar had been prepared, in every respect, for the coming of Christ. Note that Origen was the first Christian thinker to connect the birth of Christ to the *pax romana* of the Augustan age.
27 Ibid. 7.3.
28 Salv., *De gub. D.*, 7.1; see trans. Eva M. Sanford, *On the Government of God* (New York: Columbia University Press, 1930), 189; see generally, David Lambert, "The Uses of Decay: History in Salvian's *De Gubernatione Dei*," in ed. Mark Vessey and Karla Pollmann, *History, Apocalypse, and the Secular Imagination: New Essays on Augustine's City of God* (Bowling Green, OH: Philosophy Documentation Center, 1999), 115–30.
29 August., *De civ. D.*, 9.4.
30 See Cic., *Tusc.*, 4.17–20.

31 Ibid. 4.17.
32 Ibid. 4.31.
33 See, for example, Cic., *Nat. D.*, 2.62.
34 Ibid. 1.14.39–40.
35 Wetzel, *Limits of Virtue*, 99.
36 Cic., *Fin.*, 4.22–23.
37 August., *De civ. D.*, 9.4.
38 Gell., *NA*, 19; see trans. John C. Rolfe, *The Attic Nights of Aulus Gellius.* LCL 212 (Cambridge, MA: Harvard University Press, repr. 1993), 351.
39 Ibid.
40 Epict., *Disc.*, 1–4. The Discourses were transcribed from lecture notes by Epictetus' student Arrian, and only books 1–4 remain.
41 Epict., *Disc.*, 1.1.
42 Gell., *NA*, 19.
43 Ibid.; see trans. Rolfe, *The Attic Nights*, 353.
44 See Sarah Catherine Byers, *Perception, Sensibility, and Moral Motivation in Augustine: A Stoic-Platonic Synthesis* (Cambridge: Cambridge University Press: 2013), 100–1.
45 August., *De civ. D.*, 9.4. See trans. David S. Wiesen, *Saint Augustine: The City of God against the Pagans.* LCL 413 (Cambridge, MA: Harvard University Press, 1968), 165.
46 Ibid.
47 August., *De civ. D.*, 9.5.
48 See Diog. Laert., *Vit. phil.*, 116.
49 Sen., *Clem.*, 2.6.4.
50 Cic., *Tusc.*, 4.12.
51 Ibid. 3.10.
52 Byers, *Perception, Sensibility*, 68–9, 81–3.
53 August., *De civ. D.*, 9.5; Sarah Catherine Byers, "The Psychology of Compassion: Stoicism in City of God 9.5," in ed. Mark Vessey, *A Companion to Augustine* (Oxford: Wiley-Blackwell, 2012), 134.
54 August., *De civ. D*, 9.5. *Quid est autem misericordia nisi alienae miseriae quaedam in nostro corde compassio qua utique si possumus subvenire compellimur?*
55 Accessed on September 18, 2019, at https://anglosaxonpoetry. camden.rutgers.edu/dream-of-the-rood.
56 Ibid. 14.9; see trans. Levine, *The City of God.*
57 Ibid.
58 Ibid.
59 Ibid.
60 See Cic., *Nat. D.*, 1.39, discussing the Stoic Chrysippus; trans. Long and Sedley, *The Hellenistic Philosophers*, vol. 1, 323.

61 See Eusebius, *Praep. evang.*, 15.14.2, discussing the Stoic Aristocles.
62 August., *De civ. D.*, 14.9
63 Ibid.; see trans. Levine, *The City of God*, 313.
64 Ibid.
65 Ibid. 9.5.
66 See trans. Maria Boulding, *Expositions of the Psalms*, 33–50, in ed. John E. Rotelle, *The Works of Saint Augustine* (New York: New City Press, 2000), 260; Anne-Emmanuelle Ceulemans, "Instruments Real and Imaginary: Aaron's Interpretation of Isidore and an Illustrated Copy of the Toscanello," ed. Iain Fenlon, *Early Music History*, vol. 21. Studies in Medieval and Early Modern Music (Cambridge: Cambridge University Press, 2002), 13.
67 August., *En. in Ps.*, Ps. 42.5 [43]; PL 36, 479.
68 Ibid. Ps. 42.5 [43] and Ps. 32.5 [33] (2nd serm.); PL 36, 479, 280.
69 Ibid.
70 Ibid. Ps. 36.7 [37] (3rd serm.); PL 36, 388.
71 See August., *Div. quest.*, 71.2: "But he doesn't throw himself down that both lie helpless."
72 Byers, *Perception, Sensibility*, 82–3.
73 August., *De ver. rel.*, 257–8.
74 August., *Serm.*, 264, PL 38, 1213; see trans. Sr. Mary Sarah Muldowney, *Saint Augustine: Sermons on the Liturgical Seasons*. The Fathers of the Church 38 (Washington, DC: Catholic University of America Press, 1959), 398–9.

4

Remembering

As a young man, Augustine found himself propelled along a chain of haphazard desire. Tangled in his adolescent flesh, he could not distinguish "the clarity of love from the fog of lust."[1] No wonder. From the age of sixteen, when visiting the Roman baths, his desires had straightaway been nurtured and then contained by his father's expectations. "Moreover when this father of mine saw me at the baths, that I was reaching puberty and was clothed with a restless youthfulness, he, as if from this now hoping for grandchildren, was delighted to tell my mother."[2] Augustine was having none of it. His unrestrained adolescence was a lively test case for any such attempts at external control. The bathhouse episode was memorable for its merging of the various oppositions of self and other, physicality and desire, refinement and unseemliness. Miles Hollingworth has said of the event,

> Human life can be seen as remarkable for the collective loss of control that it exhibits; in the sense that our most acute discomforts are more often than not being met by an even greater degree of panic in the weird and dominating shapes of the intellectual systems of understanding. And so one form of panic is only ever handed on into another form, and something is never resolved.[3]

That is how Augustine wound up in the darkness of his physical wandering, somehow dissipating into fragments of nothingness. Each act of submission to his flesh drove him that much farther from God.

Emptiness and Desire

T. S. Eliot alluded to such unruly desire in *The Waste Land* when he spoke of coming to Carthage, the same place where Augustine had roamed and strayed. Set against the "Burning, burning, burning, burning" of the Buddha's *Fire Sermon*, it was an allusion to the Lord plucking Augustine mercifully back from the snares of beauty.[4] Not unlike the experience of the young Augustine who had yet to commit himself to God, the waste land was a place of nothingness. Without sustenance, it was barren and broken to the point that "the dead tree gives no shelter, the cricket no relief,/And the dry stone no sound of water." In this desolate world, not even the Son of man knows the truth, but approximates it virtually from "a heap of broken images." One such image is a memory of arms filled with the living potential of flowers picked as a gift from a hyacinth garden. Even this possibility for growth and regeneration cannot transcend the emptiness of nothingness. In such a place, the memory of a fertile past is synonymous with frustrated desire: "mixing/Memory and desire, stirring/Dull roots with spring rain./Winter kept us warm, covering/Earth in forgetful snow."[5] For T. S. Eliot, there is comfort in the forgetfulness of a winter that covers hope in a blanket of snow. Better to forget in this waste land than to endure the memory of unfulfilled expectation.

Augustine remembered his youth, spent as a hearer among fellow Manichaeans, as a kind of desolation. Its barrenness resided not in the failure of the Son of man to know the truth, as T. S. Eliot imagined it to be, but in his own misdirected wanderings in the physical and mental realms. With respect to the physical, Augustine tried to fill his overwhelming sense of emptiness with a love that he thirsted for as an end in itself and on its terms, without reference to God. He described the feeling like this:

> I came to Carthage, and a frying-pan of shameful loves sizzled everywhere around me. I was not in love as of yet, but I loved to be in love, and from my more hidden need, I hated myself for my rather trifling need. Loving to be in love, I looked for something I might love and I hated safety and a path without traps, because there was a hunger within me for the more interior food, for you yourself my God, yet for this hunger I was not hungry, but was without longing for the incorruptible nourishments, not because

I was filled with them, but because the emptier I was, the more I was filled with disgust.[6]

Years later, looking back on his time in Carthage, Augustine understood that the emptiness he had tried to alleviate apart from the presence of God had within it the misguided source of its continuation. He could never be filled for as long as the object of his need had been set in the wrong direction.

With respect to the mental, during his time as a Manichaean he had fallen prey to some of its fantasies, which were offered as receptacles of truth. Later, he learned these were "false bodies." "How far you are from those fantasies of mine, fantasies of bodies, which do not exist at all."[7] Because there was nothing intrinsically real about them, they were the empty casings of his desolation. "By such barrenness I was fed, but I wasn't nourished."[8] It was years later, well after his conversion, that he understood this experience with Manichaean teaching as a kind of doorway into a void. At the time, he thought he was moving toward a real and substantial truth, when, in fact, he was receding from it. For Augustine, there was something deceptive about a void you were presently inside of. Its promises lured you into the trap of thinking you were on the right track and everything was fine. For T. S. Eliot, in contrast, the disjointed narrative of modernity was the only truth worth committing to. In such a barren place, the promises of new life fell short of expectation. Those who removed the veil of self-deception ("Son of man,/You cannot say or guess...") saw this desiccation as the final vestige of a fertile past. Whereas for Augustine, memory clarifies and sharpens his perception, for the T. S. Eliot of *The Waste Land*, it disappoints.

In this chapter we shall see how memory, for Augustine, being the space in which God dwells, enables us to apprehend ourselves as a self oriented toward God, even as it liberates us temporarily from our time-bound lives. We shall see further that memory connects our present experience with similar situations and feelings we may have had in the past. The temporal separation between then and now contextualizes the sensation, while simultaneously toning it down. Detached from the intensity of the original experience, the memory cultivates the scrutiny of our emotional life, offering from this generalization of our past experiences the possibility of sympathy and compassion for others.

Movements of Time

Remembering the past for Augustine is not synonymous with reliving it or obligating oneself to continue along an established trajectory. Memory liberates because that is the space where God resides in the human mind. "Thus from the time I have learned to know you, you remain in my memory, and there I find you whenever I remember you and delight in you."[9] It allowed him to apprehend himself no longer as drowning in desire, but as oriented newly toward God. The newness resided in the endless possibilities for revision in the light of experience and emotion.

> There [in memory] also I myself meet with myself, and I recall myself, what, where, and when I have done something, and also how, when I did it, I was affected. All things that I remember are there, whether from my own experience or on the faith of others. From the same storehouse I myself out of the past weave together, at one time or another, the likenesses of things, or experiences, or beliefs, based upon things I have experienced; and from these, likewise, I infer future actions, events, and hopes, and I meditate again on all these things as if they were present.[10]

This view of memory was shaped by a flexible conception of time that circled backward and forward to encompass the experiences of the past, the here and now of the present, and the anticipation of the future. It "freed him once and for all from deterministic assumptions about the human past."[11] These are not the escapist memories of *The Waste Land*, fixed in a past that we are alienated from, and which we access only in the context of regret and disappointment. These are rather the memories of the self remaking itself in the light of the past, and in the hope of the future, and always in reference to God.

The fluid unfolding of memory is the space where Augustine met himself as an autobiographical self that intersected with the mind of God. As secure as he was in this insight, it presented him with a conceptual challenge. The common perception then, as now, was that memories evolved sequentially over the course of time and are accessed through a consecutive timeline. According to this view, the past remains in the past, never to be accessed again; the future is something to be imagined that has not yet taken place; and the present unfolds without our mental efforts. This is the linear conception of time that the Egyptian Greek poet Constantine Cavafy (d. 1933) would later speak of: "The days of our future stand before us/like a row of little lighted candles—/golden, warm, and lively little candles./The days gone by remain behind us, a mournful line of burnt-out candles...I do not want to turn back, lest I see and shudder—/how quickly the somber line lengthens,/how quickly the burnt-out candles multiply."[12] In this view of time we are connected to the past only through our sorrow for its absence, and to the future through our longing for its presence.

Augustine challenged the common perception by rethinking our assumptions about the nature of time and how it operates. Upon closer inspection, he found that time does not truly exist in the sense of having a discernible reality apart from the conventions ascribed to it. There is a distinction between the events themselves, which happened at some point now in the past, and the remembering of those events, which always takes place in the present. "For example, my childhood, which is not now, in time past is, which [time] is not now; but its image, when I recall and narrate it, I consider in present time, because it is still in my memory."[13] When accessing memories, it was not as if an event from the past had been taken from a storehouse of events that then reentered the mind. Remembering the past did not, after all, require him to relive it, for there was a difference between the past as it happened at some time not now present, and the recollection of the past in the present.

For Augustine, the difference between the original experience, now in the past, and the memory of it, now present, unfolded in the realm of the senses. That is where he thought the content of our lives was processed into images that recorded the past as something having already taken place. Shaped by the senses, this experience of the past was always a present awareness. In such a temporal system, where the past existed provisionally in the present, the future was not all that different from the past. Even though the events of the future had not yet occurred, its images could be conceived in the mind in the present as something about to take place. We experience the future, which is not yet real, as a time that can be foretold from things in the present, as if it were real. "Future things are, therefore, not yet, and if they are not yet, they do not exist, and if they do not exist, they cannot be seen at all; but they can be foretold by things in the present, which already exist and are already seen."[14] This notion of a "prior and future time" was the result of what we might call a "temporal dispersion," which Augustine envisioned like this: an image is formed in the mind as a trace from the past, or as foresight from the future, that has moved through our senses. Memories, as well as predictions, consist of words that are then conceived from these images. Any time that is "not yet now" is several steps removed from the things being thought of. Events not in the present have already passed through the senses and left traces on the mind. There they form images that are conceived from, and articulated into, words.

The ongoing passage of our lives through the filter of our senses imparts time with an experiential dimension. It confirmed for Augustine that nothing was objectively real about the movement of time through the times we conventionally refer to as past, present, and future. Time, in the sequential form he knew it, was really just an image in our present mind of something that either was, or was about to be. As Augustine put it, "an improper custom" spoke of past and future as if they had being now. "These three indeed exist somehow in the mind, and elsewhere I do not see them; the present of past things is memory, the present of present things is mental contemplation, and the present of future things is expectation."[15] The only time he knew in the present was the moment that was passing away.

For Augustine, this raised the related problems of the duration of moments in time and their measurement. Since the present was always in flux, there was no way to determine when a moment became the past or when it extended into the future:

> How do we truly measure the present time when it has no space? We measure it, therefore, while it passes, but when it has past, we do not measure it, for it does not exist to be measured. But from where, and which way, and to where does it pass when it is being measured? From where, unless from the future? Which way, unless through the present? To where, unless into the past?[16]

The present moment, being the only time he could grasp, always threatened to elude him. On the verge of becoming the past—which was really something else—the present could scarcely be measured before it slipped away. In that sense, Augustine could not quantify securely what even the present time consisted in.

Real and Subjective Time

Augustine's personal experience of time before and after his conversion offered a partial solution. We have already seen that he, while still a Manichaean, grieved the death of his friend by substituting moments from the past, which in the process of remembering evoked sadness, with the present moments he shared with friends. The new experiences were supposed to replace the painful images of his deceased friend with a different set of joyful images. It was as if his new friends recorded over the tracks of his mind to erase certain vestiges of a past he did not wish to remember. At the same time, he had longed to relive his memories so as to experience a delicious kind of sadness. The inherent contradiction of his emotional life—as he both wallowed in and wished to escape from his memories—made him realize that the life he had lived prior to his conversion had been a series of fragmentary moments. Disconnected from the narrative of salvation, he had drifted from one moment to the next, aimlessly weaving his story together according to the ebb and flow of his desires. His pre-conversion self had been driven by narcissism.

After his conversion, Augustine experienced a different sense of time with his mother at Ostia, shortly before she died.[17] While overlooking a garden in the courtyard of the house they were staying in, they shared a moment of deep contemplation. It was based on their longing to know the eternal fountain of life. In a kind of mystical ascent that took place in stages, they contemplated the heavenly bodies and the beauty of God's works in the context of their interior reflections. The final stage of contemplation transcended their minds to arrive at "the region of continuous abundance, where you feed Israel forever with the true food, and where life is the wisdom through which all these things are made, both which have been and which will be."[18] Here in the space of eternal wisdom they lingered for a while in timeless contemplation. "This wisdom is not made, but is thus, as it was, and so it will always be, or rather, it is not in it to be as it was and will be, but only to be, because it is eternal."[19] In defiance of linear time, the wisdom they had a glimpse of was not subject to anything they recognized as change. After this temporal suspension, they returned then to the sequential mode of self-expression using words that had a "beginning and ending."

A conversation ensued in which they considered whether this single "moment of understanding (*momentum intellegentiae*)" that they had shared might, if it were extended indefinitely, be the equivalent of existing eternally within the Lord. The moment had been unlike any other he had experienced. It neither faded into the past, nor anticipated the future. Although it was fleeting, for the length of its stay it resided in the mental contemplation of the present. In the context of its unfolding, the moment could not be measured. It was the perfect manifestation of the silencing of the self to the self, which ushered in the eternal Word of God. "If the mind itself be silent to itself, if all dreams and imaginary revelations be silent, if every tongue and every sign and whatever passes away be utterly silent to anyone," it might be possible to exist within "the joy of the Lord."[20] In silence, the soul discarded its worldly accumulations and became what it was supposed to be prior to the Fall.

For Augustine, the silence and stability of deep contemplation was opposed thoroughly to the loudness and fluidity of the world. It was the difference between the life he called a "distention (*distentio*)," which was spread out over time, filled with the multiplicity of our changing attention,[21] and the soul that was *extentus*, literally "stretched" and attracted into a timeless present.[22] "Let them stretch toward those things that exist before and understand that you, the eternal creator of all times, existed before all times and that no times are co-eternal with you."[23] Whereas this life was dispersed along the time-bound occupations of past, present, and future, a timeless extension pulled the soul toward the stillness of contemplation. There was only the slightest connection with the neoplatonism of Plotinus, who spoke of time, in its essential characteristics, as a continuous (*adiastaton*) movement of the soul that can never be broken apart or scattered into measurable segments.[24] Augustine would object to the scattering of time, its dispersal among a fragmented self, in reflecting upon his experiences as a young man.

Augustine knew that God's time was different. It was not spread out or fractured along the continuum of a narrative arc we ourselves devised. It did not remember a past that was no longer real, or hope for a future to propose another version of the present possibilities. Nor was it the eternal present that T. S. Eliot imagined in the *Four Quartets*. "Time present and time past/Are both perhaps present in time future,/And time future contained in time past./If all time is eternally present/All time is unredeemable./What might have been is an abstraction/Remaining a perpetual possibility/Only in a world of speculation./What might have been and what has been/Point to one end, which is always present." For Augustine, the eternal present of God's time retains the difference between "what might have been" and "what has been." "What might have been" is the life of human beings without the Fall. "What has been" is the act of disobedience that took place in the garden. For T. S. Eliot, the garden is really just a mirage, like the rose-garden that never really was: "Footfalls echo in the memory/Down the passage which we did not take/Towards the door we never opened/Into the rose-garden." The possibility of it having existed can be recalled only in the narrative of a time past and a time future that never truly are. "To be conscious," and, therefore, to be present, "is not to be in time." This was Eliot's way of removing us from the timeline of our disobedience and into the timeless incoherence of hopelessness.

God's time is always the present, though not in the sense that T. S. Eliot described. It is a vision of simultaneity that sees every past event we put into sequence and every future event we imagine as potentially happening now. It does not deny our past as not having happened, or the possibility of our future as just a dream. Donald L. Ross put it like this:

> Now for Augustine time considered in itself is merely a dimension of reality; it is non-sequential. It is the sequentiality of time, not time itself, that is a psychological phenomenon. God, being outside time, views it as it really is, in a non-sequential fashion, spread out like space to his eternal gaze. The human mind, however, is condemned to sequential experience, even though time as it is in itself is a dimension without sequence.[25]

Through contemplation, the soul extends beyond the multiplicity and dispersal of this world into a timeless present. It mirrors God's perception of time as a nonsequential spreading-out across the dimension of space. It lets go of the past and postpones the future to experience the present as the only time that really is. This was the moment of suspended contemplation Augustine experienced with his mother at Ostia. It lasted only for a moment. He knew there was nothing to undo forever the perception of his traveling through time consecutively.

Augustine was puzzled by the movement from eternal time, which he had experienced briefly at Ostia, to the sequential time he knew from daily life. Unsettled by the shift, he identified several focal points to help him make sense of the distinction. First, whereas God existed outside of time and made the heaven and earth "free from times," neither heaven nor earth—as a part of God's creation—was coeternal with God. Yet being "free from times," heaven and earth were detached from the consecutive unfolding of time that we ourselves are bound to.[26] As cosmic bodies, they formed a kind of intermediary between God's eternal present and our experience of linear time. Poised between two times, heaven and earth knew of time as it really was, "not in part, not darkly, not in a glass, but all at once, clearly, face to face, not in this way now and in that way then, but, as I said, simultaneously, without any vicissitude of times."[27] Just as heaven knew all things at once, without the "vicissitude of times," so did earth, in its original state of formlessness. Augustine found it significant that both had been made prior to any scriptural mention of the consecutive time it spoke of as "days."

Second, when God spoke creation into existence through God's Word, one word did not follow upon the next in sequence. In other words, the temporal restrictions of human speech did not function: "for that which was spoken was not finished and another thing spoken until all things could be said, but all at once and eternally."[28] The Word that created the world was, therefore, different from the disembodied voice that uttered the words recorded in Scripture, "You are my beloved Son."[29] For Augustine, that disembodied voice had a beginning and ending, its syllables made a sound and then passed by, "the second after the first, the third after the second, and so on in order, until the last came after the rest, and silence after the last."[30] This was God speaking in the language of consecutive speech to accommodate our rhythms. It was a provisional form of communication to convey God's will to time-bound human beings. "The exterior ear announced these words of yours, made at the time, to the intelligent mind, whose interior ear has been set for your eternal Word." Augustine was aware of an inner wisdom we possess that distinguishes God's temporal words from the eternal

Word in its resounding silence. Held deep within our mind, this wisdom guides us across the divide between the sequential time we live in and God's time, where the human experience of past, present, and future are present simultaneously in an eternal instant.

Third, it followed that God moved and spoke in two different ways. There was the extension of time that God adapted to our life experiences and spoke in occasionally, and there was the Word that spoke creation into existence before time began. This distinction in God's mode of speech bridged the gap that human beings experienced between the sequential unfolding of time and its eternal counterpart. We have seen in the context of Augustine's mourning for his friend that consecutive time, when left to its devices, reduced human beings to their momentary lives of desperation. Living from one disconnected moment to the next was the truncated experience of time Augustine had experienced prior to his conversion. He had soothed his pain by introducing new experiences to record over the old.

Through the practice of contemplation he learned to halt this process of momentary substitution and make time stand still in the eternal presence of God. His new perception of time let him glimpse the truth of divine love, the permanence and principles of which operate outside of temporal limitation. This was the experience of the timeless moment of contemplation he shared with his mother at Ostia. Such an extension of the soul across the dimensions of space and time was similar to, and deliberately evoked, the simultaneity of God's time, which functioned on its terms and without sequential restrictions. Everything God spoke through God's coeternal Word was spoken at the same time and definitively forever. Truly this was the simultaneous and all-at-once expression of God's creative act that was, by definition, timeless. It defied the movement of things past that no longer were, and of things present that had once not been. It challenged the rising and passing of one moment to the next that circumscribed our mortal lives.

Finally, the paradox of time was apparent to Augustine in the motion of the heavenly bodies. Though eternal in its essence, time was perceived by human beings sequentially. This was the case even when observing such bodies as the sun that seemed to move independently of our perception. Whereas certain ancient philosophers, such as Plato, had equated time with cosmic movement, Augustine knew that time operated distinctly. Like Aristotle, he understood that time was not synonymous with motion, but was an attribute of motion. With respect to the heavenly bodies, this meant that time was the measurement of change. "When a body is set in motion, I, by time, measure how long it may have moved, from which point it began to be moved, until it ceased."[31] The same conclusions he had drawn from examining his memories and his sense of himself as extended over time also applied here. Time as a function of measurement did not have independent existence. It was not "the motion of a body," but a *distentio* stretched into temporality,[32] even when its properties were used to access the seemingly timeless motions of the heavenly spheres.[33]

Memories of Feelings

The insight that time is an attribute of change was relevant for understanding more than simply the motions of heavenly bodies. It applied as well to Augustine's deepening sense of his emotional memories changing over the course of time, while remaining somehow independent of time. He noticed that the memory of certain emotions he had felt in the past often differed from his initial experience. The difference related to the boundary he observed in our emotional life, which separated the emotion contained in the memory of a feeling from the past, from the feeling itself that was contained in the mind (*animus*). The latter is what we might call a primary emotional experience, while the memory of it is a second-order reflection.

The process of reflecting upon the past and remembering it also triggered certain associations that evoked new feelings out of the old. Remembering how we felt in some prior time does not oblige us to relive that prior time, or even to feel those same emotions. Cavafy said it like this: "Ideal and dearly beloved voices/of those who are dead, or of those/who are lost to us like the dead./Sometimes they speak to us in our dreams; sometimes in thought the mind hears them./And for a moment with their echo other echoes/return from the first poetry of our lives—/like music that extinguishes the far-off night."[34] These new emotions, which emerge from the old, are the "music that extinguishes the far-off night" to form new echoes in our lives. They are the feelings we have about our feelings, as well as the feelings that arise in the temporal context of our present recollections and of the time that has passed between then and now. As Augustine put it,

> For though I am not joyful, I remember myself to have been joyful, and though I am not sad, I recall my past sadness, and that I have been afraid at some time or other I recall without fear, and I am mindful of a former desire, without desire. Sometimes, on the contrary, I remember my past sadness full of joy, and my joy with sadness.[35]

For Augustine, the emotions he felt over the course of time did not merge one into the other. Time reshaped the emotions, but did not blur them into a haze. They retained their distinction enough to show how time had altered their expression. Yet the method of this transformation was puzzling to Augustine. If the mind was one thing and the memory another, and they held their state of separation, then how, he wondered, could a feeling stored in the mind be recalled at will and newly formed, while still being reminiscent of what he had felt before?

Related to this was the problem of containment. How could feelings he had felt in the past be contained thoroughly in the memory without their surfacing against his will in the present? It was as if his feelings were stored in a file to be opened and closed either according to his desire to remember, or in the context of certain conditions and circumstances that evoked how he had felt in the past. "The memory was, therefore, without a doubt like the stomach of the mind, and joy and sadness truly like sweet and sour meat." Like an emotional storage space, memory was a container that related to, but remained separate from, mind. Just as the stomach stores food without our tasting it, so the memory stores emotions without our feeling them repeatedly. Although the metaphor evoked an aspect of memory, it did not account for certain traumatic memories in which feelings cannot be contained without feeling them and often flow uncontrollably. Augustine had experienced the permeability of his emotional life when dealing with the death of his friend. No matter where he went, the memory of the time they had spent in this or that place triggered feelings he wished to suppress.

There was another kind of memory that pertained to the emotions, but in a different way. Whereas the memory (*recognitio* and *memoria*) of emotions he had felt before initiated a comparison with, and reassessment of, his current emotional life, their recollection (*recordatio*), strictly speaking, did not move him. For instance, in recollection, he was able to bring forth from his memory the four perturbations of the soul, i.e., desire, joy, fear, and sorrow, without calling to mind "the sweetness of joy" or "the bitterness of sorrow." It was the difference between evaluating his feelings with reference to the past—noticing how they may or may not have changed over the course of time—and the mechanics of recollection. The former involved his memory, while the latter retrieved the contents of intellectual knowledge he had acquired through his efforts. It meant that his knowledge of the soul's perturbations had come to him through the philosophical trajectory of the Stoics, for example, and not from his autobiographical experience.

Aristotle similarly had distinguished the memory of something that happened in the past from its recollection. Julia Annas has said, "[Recollection] is not *of the past* in the way that memory is. Aristotle never says that it is and it has no characteristics that make it likely that it is. It is recovery of past knowledge, but it lacks those features of memory which make the past acquiring of knowledge part of what is remembered."[36] Augustine started out more like Plato than Aristotle, however. Jaroslav Pelikan has remarked, "In his early Neoplatonic discourses, especially *On the teacher* [*De magistro*], Augustine spoke of memory as an 'inner word' of recollection—a reminiscence of the Platonic doctrine of the preexistence of the soul, trailing clouds of glory."[37] It was only later that he "attribute[d] this recollection to 'the disposition of the Creator' rather than to preexistence, and thus [paid] more attention to the empirical basis of memory."[38]

Augustine's treatise *On Music* (*c*.387–391) was an important step along this trajectory. In it, the soul is said to receive all its motions and make them subject to recall by the force of memory.[39] There are carnal memories, spiritual memories, memories that form out of images of things we have seen and known, and memories of things we have only imagined—often incorrectly—from what we have seen and known. The challenge is to isolate the spiritual motions of the soul from every lower-order thing that might oppress it. This is how we arrive at the memory of truth. It is a fundamental orientation that entails loving God and fellow souls as yourself.[40] As Paige E. Hochschild has remarked, remembering truth is like remembering the principles by which we judge the distinctive equality and ratio that *characterize* a pleasing and correct rhythm. Augustine compares this to remembering a truth such as "two and two make four"; it is truth about which, if knowledge is verily present, there can be no uncertainty. And this kind of truth, Augustine concludes, is properly *in* the soul, though *from* God who is truth most supremely.[41]

The difference between Augustine's memory of his emotions and his initial experience of them raises similar issues with respect to truth and authenticity. If remembering truth is like remembering the essential principles of beauty and rhythm, then remembering emotions that change over time poses a challenge. The absence of continuity and sameness called into question the authenticity of his emotional life.[42]

Augustine found his resolution in the workings of our mind, which contain not only "the sounds of the names according to the images imprinted on it by the bodily senses, but [where] we also find the conceptions of the things (*notiones rerum*) themselves, which we did not receive through any door of the flesh, but which the mind (*animus*) itself perceiving by the experience of its own passions committed to memory."[43] The memory of how we felt at some prior point in our lives involves more than just assigning a name to an emotional experience that we later recollect when we wish to. Whereas such feelings as joy, sorrow, grief, and fear are triggered by a sensory experience at the outset, their recollection taps into the principle that defines their truth. This is what Augustine meant when he spoke of the *notiones rerum*, the "conceptions of things." These conceptions (*notiones*) and mental impressions (*notationes*) are the avenues through which emotions enter the mind.[44] Cicero had used the same expression to describe the innate discernment of certain fundamental virtues that are synonymous with truth.[45]

Augustine did not relive the feelings he remembered, because what he remembered was not the bodily experience but the underlying conception that the *animus* perceived "by the experience of its own passions." The mind abstracted the essence of the emotional experience, which it stored "in the belly of the mind" until it retrieved the feeling later. The secondary feelings Augustine felt about his feelings were experienced and then retained according to a similar mental process.

The memory of his emotions was not unlike his memory of absent things. During the night, for example, he remembered the sun by accessing the image of it he held in his memory. No longer present, the sun existed only as an image in his mind. For Augustine, the emotions functioned similarly. "I name a bodily pain, yet it is not present to me when there is no pain; unless, however, its image had been in my memory, I wouldn't know what I should say, nor would I, in discussing [the matter], [be able to] distinguish it from pleasure."[46] Although the emotion he had felt in the past was gone, the image of it was retained in the memory for his recollection. This is where his emotional life deviated from his memory of objects and other such things. The difference between feeling the pain at some time in the past and remembering it in an altered form was almost like forgetting. The experience of pain was not reactivated every time he thought of it. Like T. S. Eliot's, "Footfalls [that] echo in the memory/Down the passage which we did not take/Towards the door we never opened/Into the rose-garden," it was as if the pain had never happened. It was just a lingering possibility.

The memory of his emotions, more than any other memory, allowed Augustine to experience the temporal difference between then and now without being deceived into thinking that time was something real. He knew that time was a function of change and had no eternal existence. Yet his emotional variation unfolded in the passage of time as a kind of silence, a "privation of memory" that shared its message by pointing to what was no longer there. It was the sign that

> pretend[ed] not to be a sign…a sign that affects to be the negation of representation, to be the absence of a sign; it is a sign that suggests and evokes without actually representing. So to the extent that it is the object of perception, silence carries connotations of dissimulation. It implies an absence of some kind—something that might be said, a sound that might be made, but is not.[47]

For Augustine, a feeling from the past is a sign that signifies through an absence that exists paradoxically in his recollection. There is even the sense that if he were to feel the pain he had felt in the past, it would no longer be recollecting. It would be like experiencing it as a new sensation in the present.

Closeness Out of Distance

Temporally removed from the initial experience, the act of remembering his emotions let Augustine contemplate and speak of painful sensations and occurrences from the past without feeling them again. The insight had ramifications well beyond a theory of memory. The temporal and spatial distance inherent in the process of remembering also addressed the moral shortcomings Augustine perceived in the Stoic wise man. Dedicated to his self-imposed constraints, the wise man worried more about preserving emotional tranquility than he did about engaging compassionately with other people's suffering. We have already seen how sternly Augustine criticized the trembling wise man for preferring his personal safety to the moral virtue of another human being. Whereas lingering in his own pain was morally questionable, feeling someone else's would have been consistent with upholding compassion as a Christian virtue. "What is compassion (*misericordia*)," asked Augustine, "but a kind of sympathy (*compassio*) in our heart for the suffering (*miseria*) of another that surely compels us to help as much as we can?"[48]

There is yet more to the story. In his early years, Augustine had been worried about the possibility of compassion fatigue. This is the feeling of emotional exhaustion that comes with involving yourself emotionally with other people's suffering. There is always the concern that some might avoid the emotional distress altogether by refusing to assist the needy.[49] One solution is to encourage people to strike a balance between sharing in the suffering of another and maintaining the appropriate emotional distance to prevent them both from becoming miserable. "He doesn't throw himself down that both lie helpless."[50] As Raymond Canning has said, "The sage's 'freedom from all distress'…has to be read with the nuance 'freedom from all distress that would cripple him and make him ineffectual on behalf of others.'"[51] Another solution was there already for Augustine in the "fields, caves, and caverns" of his memory, where "conceptions and mental impressions" are formed of the "affections of his mind."[52] Even unpleasant feelings, such as suffering, are retained in the various mental receptacles there among the "innumerably full, innumerable kinds of things."[53] When such feelings are recalled later, they are subject then to the moderating influence of time.

This suggests that the same mechanism that soothes our emotional response to the past also modulates the feelings we feel on behalf of another and similarly calms our response. In spite of the emotional distance, a connection persists between us and the person suffering. Providing the space in which compassion comes alive, the connection preserves certain boundaries while it threatens to break them down. In the absence of such boundaries, there would have been only the shared feeling of suffering, with no reflection upon its meaning, or possibility for its transformation into something tangible that heals. I have already shown that, for Augustine, feeling merely what the other person feels does not generate compassion inevitably. The connection between the self and the other must produce some sort of charitable action. For this to happen, the emotional response to the person suffering should be regulated and its intensity diminished.

During the process of emotional separation and connection, the exercise of the imagination comes into play. With respect to separation, David Hume (d. 1776), the philosopher of the Scottish Enlightenment, for example, believed that feeling pity for someone else's suffering does not depend upon the object of pity feeling miserable herself. This scenario is meant to account for the unusual circumstance in which the person apparently suffering has become so accustomed to her plight that she no longer wishes to alleviate it. With respect to connection, the French philosopher Jean-Jacques Rousseau thought that the feelings we sense in those who suffer determine the extent to which we pity them. The imagination functions for each philosopher according to the way in which the experience of shared suffering is comprehended. Whereas for Hume the imagination reconstructs what the other person might have felt had she been aware of her plight, for Rousseau the imagination dissolves the boundaries between the self and the other, which then carries the person compassionately into the realm of the other person.[54] It is the difference between recreating the experience of the sufferer, as in Hume, and penetrating that experience, as in Rousseau.

Neither for Rousseau nor for Augustine does the shared experience of suffering involve a breakdown of individuality. In the spirit of Paul, Augustine envisioned the church of all those who believe in Christ as a unified body, joined by the Holy Spirit:

> We are in one body, we have one head, in heaven. Brothers, our two eyes do not see each other, just as they do not know each other. But do they not know each other in the charity of the bodily composition? For, that you may know that in the joining together of charity they do know each other, [consider that] when both eyes are open, the right may not rest on some object, on which the left eye does not also rest. Direct the glance of the right eye without the other, if you can. Together they meet, together they are directed. Their purpose is one, but their positions are diverse.[55]

Caritas binds the members of the body of Christ into a common love and shared objective, while maintaining their uniqueness. For compassion to thrive, it is necessary to discern where one person's suffering begins and the other person's ends. Its greatest aspiration is to share the *viscera dilectionis*, the "innermost aspects of love,"[56] while preserving the distinction between the self and the other. There is no sense here of communal dissolution.

Adam Smith, the philosopher of the Scottish Enlightenment, developed a similar theory in ways that are relevant to, and implicitly build upon, Augustine. As it was for Augustine, imagining what the other person might be feeling shaped his understanding of pity: "[it is] the emotion that we feel for the misery of others, either when we see or are made to conceive of it in a very lively manner."[57] He developed this imaginative reconstruction of the other person's feelings in his theory of the judicious spectator. The spectator is the idealized observer who studies our distress in meticulous detail, judges the legitimacy of our suffering by imagining himself in similar circumstances, and determines whether and the extent to which his sympathy for our plight is warranted. He is like an impartial fact-gatherer specializing in the minutiae of our emotional lives. The process is impartial because it thrives on the distance we travel in the solitude of our emotional lives. Although the spectator is sympathetic, he does not surrender himself to the other person's suffering. "The thought of their safety, the thought that they are not the sufferer, continually intrudes upon them."[58]

The emotional difference the spectator observes between himself and the other person should not be ascribed to any imaginative shortcomings. To the contrary, a lively imagination is essential to coming to terms compassionately with human suffering. It is the space in which compassion thrives. The reciprocal relationship between the spectator and the sufferer unfolds like this: just as the spectator immerses himself in the feeling of distress, he returns to his position of security by "the secret consciousness" that the change in circumstance is merely imaginary. The person suffering experiences then the cooled-down sympathy of the spectator and reevaluates his personal distress, "flatten[ing] his emotions so that they are in nearer harmony to those who are around him."[59] A therapeutic effect occurs that lets the sufferer see himself through the detached eyes of the spectator. As "the sufferer learns to watch himself as the spectator would," the sympathy of the spectator and the distress of the sufferer begin to subside in equal measure.[60] Whereas empathy—feeling the same thing the other person feels— reproduces the original pain, compassion modifies it and, in the process, tones it down. By continually monitoring our emotional response to other people's suffering, we develop a deepening awareness of who we are as sympathetic human beings.[61]

Emotional distance is similarly relevant to Augustine's understanding of compassion. The shared feeling of suffering he encouraged was never supposed to become so overwhelming that we mistake someone else's unhappiness for our own. There was, in other words, no sense in falling down that both become helpless.[62] The sympathy in the heart that Augustine spoke of has nothing to do with emotional contagion. There is a limit to the depth of emotion we are supposed to display with respect to other people's suffering. This subtle detachment should not be confused with insensitivity:

> But as long as we bear the weakness of this life, then we live rather un-righteously if we have none of these [feelings] at all. For the apostle disparaged and denounced some whom he said were without feeling (Romans 1:31). The sacred psalms also reproached those of whom it says, "I looked for some to lament with me, and there was none." For to feel no pain at all while we are in this place of misery "surely takes place," as one of our worldly men of letters has said, stating, "not without the great price of cruelty in the soul and of insensitivity in the body."[63]

It is rather the tempered expression of sympathy that draws upon the perception of shared experience. For Augustine, this perception resides in the vastness of memory. We have seen that remembering emotions over the course of time creates a distance between then and now that allows us to engage with memories from our past without reliving the pain.

The model applies to our engagement with human experiences more generally. As we remember feelings we felt at some time in our past, we tap into the storehouse of vital experiences that have shaped the contours of our lives: "I come to the fields and spacious chambers of my memory, where [I find] the treasures of countless images, carried into it from all kinds of things [perceived] by the senses."[64] From this storehouse, we build bridges to other people's lives. The shift from remembering our experiences to considering someone else's takes place in the connection between memory and imagination. Todd Breyfogle has said, "Imagination, then, 'fills gaps' so to speak in the memory by picturing what one can expect in the future. Imagination thus has a creative power. From images in memory, imagination creates new images which reside in memory."[65] The same processes that apply to imagining future events also apply to picturing other people's experiences. We fill gaps in our memory by imagining what other people might be feeling.

The philosopher and ethicist Martha C. Nussbaum has similarly shown how necessary the imagination is for compassion to flourish. With the help of a fertile imagination, those whose experiences differ from ours become real human beings to whom we are capable of becoming emotionally attached.[66] These people whose lives are nothing like our own, and whose circumstances we are unlikely to share, enter into what Nussbaum has called our "circle of concern." It is the ever-widening orbit that contains whatever we love. A sadness we feel for an earthquake victim from the other side of the world, for example, imparts to us the emotional information we need to determine that a person who was remote from our life has somehow been woven into its fabric. It is the work of the imagination that allows this to happen. The feeling might even prompt us to act should we become sufficiently unsettled.

For Nussbaum, our emotions are "suffused with intelligence and discernment" and contain "in themselves an awareness of value or importance." As such, they impart information relevant to forming ethical judgments.[67] They tell us what we care about. This cognitive model of our emotional life rejects implicitly the ideal of the Stoic wise person, whom Augustine criticized for preferring his own safety to the moral and physical welfare of other human beings. This same Stoic indifference to human suffering has, nevertheless, been absorbed into the Western philosophical tradition, where it has been upheld as the pinnacle of our emotional aspirations. Under such a model, other-regarding emotions become synonymous with sentimental weakness. Because there is no perceived value in their expression, they become associated with irrationality. This is the philosophical trajectory that Nussbaum and the theologian Oliver Davies, for instance, have reconsidered and set on a new course. Emotions are not irrational eruptions of feeling that undermine the cool and calculated reflections of reason, but are valuable judgments that let us know what is necessary for our flourishing.[68]

Similar to Augustine, Nussbaum views compassion as a decision to act on behalf of another human being whose suffering has evoked our sympathy and whose life and well-being we have placed within our circle of concern. The circle is enriched with the "treasures of countless images" that Augustine spoke of, and is filled with such memories. Whereas for Nussbaum, our emotions are structured cognitively, and function as such in our lives, for Augustine, they are cognitive while being subject to fluctuation, second-order reflection, and reevaluation over time.[69] For Augustine, remembering our emotions tends to cool them down. This is similar to the judicious spectator, described by Adam Smith, who sympathizes with another person's suffering and then evaluates it objectively. The detached coolness of the spectator serves the interests of the person suffering by moderating her emotional response.

For Augustine, this sense of emotional remove is not unlike the temporal distance over the course of which the memory of our emotional life unfolds. The difference between how we felt then and how we feel now provides the neutral space in which we evaluate emotional intensity in order to quiet it down. The process of emotional modulation encourages sympathy and makes it possible for it to flourish, while respecting the integrity of individual boundaries. It makes the emotional lives of others, which cannot be felt directly through our bodily senses, relevant and manageable.

Notes

1   August., *Conf.*, 2.2.1.
2   Ibid. 2.3.6.
3   Hollingworth, *Saint Augustine of Hippo*, 86.
4   The juxtaposition with Augustine was, in the words of T. S. Eliot, not an accident. See August., *Conf.*, 3.1; 10.34.
5   T. S. Eliot, *The Waste Land*, I: "The Burial of the Dead."
6   August., *Conf.*, 3.1.
7   Ibid. 3.6.
8   Ibid.
9   Ibid. 10.24.
10 Ibid. 10.8; see trans. Watts, *Confessions*, 99.
11 Paul J. Archambault, "Augustine, Memory, and the Development of Autobiography," *Augustinian Studies* 13 (1982): 23–30.
12 Constantine Cavafy, *Candles*.
13 August., *Conf.*, 11.18; trans. Watts, *Confessions*, 249.
14 Ibid; trans. Watts, *Confessions*, 251.
15 Ibid. 11.20; see trans. Watts, *Confessions*, 250.
16 Ibid. 11.21; see trans. Watts, *Confessions*, 255.
17 See my *Passion and Compassion in Early Christianity* (Cambridge: Cambridge University Press, 2016), 104–5.
18 August., *Conf.*, 9.10; See trans. Watts, *Confessions*, 49.
19 Ibid; trans. Watts, *Confessions*, 49.
20 August., *Conf.*, 9.10; See trans. Watts, *Confessions*, 51.
21 A reference to Rowan Williams, *On Augustine* (London: Bloomsbury, 2016), 2.
22 August., *Conf.*, 11.29, in which Augustine differentiates "distentus (spread out)" from "extentus (extended or attracted)." See David van Dusen, *Space of Time: Sensualist Interpretation of Time in Augustine, Confessions 10 to 12* (Leiden: Brill, 2014), 17: *distentio* "depicts not a contraction, intention, or recoil, but a dilation, refraction and spatialization of the soul." For van Dusen, the body facilitates the soul's *distentio* through the corporeal experience of sense, allowing the soul to experience time.
23 Ibid. 11.30; trans. Watts, *Confessions*, 281.
24 Plotinus, *Enn.*, 3.7.13. Note that Plotinus' Greek verb, *diaspao*, meaning "to scatter" or "break apart," can also be used metaphorically, like Augustine's Latin noun *distentio*, to mean "distract."
25 Donald L. Ross, "Time, the Heaven of Heavens, and Memory in Augustine's *Confessions*," *Augustinian Studies* 22 (1991): 191–205 (196).

26   Ibid. 198.
27   August., *Conf.*, 12.13; trans. Watts, *Confessions*, 313.
28   August., *Conf.*, 11.7; see trans. Watts, *Confessions*, 225.
29   Ibid. 11.6, citing Mt. 3:17.
30   Ibid; trans. Watts, *Confessions*, 229.
31   August., *Conf.*, 11.24; see trans. Watts, *Confessions*, 263.
32   Ibid. 11.23.
33   August., *Conf.*, 11.24.
34   Constantine Cavafy, *Voices*.
35   August., *Conf.*, 10.14; see trans. Watts, *Confessions*, 111.
36   Julia Annas, "Aristotle on Memory and the Self," *Oxford Studies in Ancient Philosophy* 4 (1986): 99–117 (113).
37   Jaroslav Pelikan, *The Mystery of Continuity: Time and History, Memory and Eternity in the Thought of St. Augustine* (Charlottesville: University Press of Virginia, 1986), 25.
38   Ibid.
39   August., *De mus.*, 6.11.31.
40   Ibid. 6.14.46.
41   Paige E. Hochschild, *Memory in Augustine's Theological Anthropology* (Oxford: Oxford University Press, 2012), 129.
42   Augustine does not make this point explicitly.
43   August., *Conf.*, 10.14; trans. Watts, *Confessions*, 115.
44   Ibid. 10.17.
45   Cic., *Tusc.*, 5.39.114.
46   August., *Conf.*, 10.15; see trans. Watts, *Confessions*, 115.
47   Charles W. Hedrick, *History and Silence: Purge and Rehabilitation of Memory in Late Antiquity* (Austin: University of Texas Press, 2000), 120.
48   August., *De civ. D.*, 9.5. *Quid est autem misericordia nisi alienae miseriae quaedam in nostro corde compassio qua utique si possumus subvenire compellimur?*
49   August., *De mor. Eccl. cath.*, 1.27.53; see my *Passion and Compassion*, 113–114.
50   August., *Div. quest.*, 71.2; cited by Raymond Canning, "Augustine on the Identity of the Neighbour and the Meaning of True Love for Him 'as ourselves' (Matt. 22.39) and 'as Christ has loved us' (Jn. 13.34)," *Augustiniana* 36 (1986): 161–239 (179).
51   Ibid. See also August., *Conf.*, 3.2.2–4.
52   August., *Conf.*, 10.17.
53   Ibid.
54   Rousseau, *Émile*, 223.

55 August., *In Iohan. ep.*, 6.10; PL 35, 2025, lines 47–55; see trans. Rev. H. Browne, *St. Augustin: Ten Homilies on the First Epistle of John.* NPNF 7 (Edinburgh: T&T Clark, repr. 1991), 498.

56 Ibid. 6.2.

57 Smith, *Moral Sentiments*, 13.

58 Ibid. 28.

59 Ibid.

60 Ibid. 29

61 Fonna Forman-Barzilai, "Sympathy in Spaces: Adam Smith on Proximity," *Political Theory* 33, no. 2 (2005): 189–217 (195–6). As she puts it, "discipline takes place under surveillance and chisels the social beings we become." Ibid. 196.

62 See above, August., *Div. quest.*, 71.2.

63 August., *De civ. D.*, 14.9; Levine, *The City of God*, 313, 312 n. 3 ("Crantor, cited by Cicero, *Tusc.* 3.6.12.").

64 August., *Conf.*, 10.8; see trans. Watts, *Confessions*, 93–5.

65 Todd Breyfogle, "Memory and the Imagination in Augustine's Confessions," *New Blackfriars* 75, 881 (1994): 210–23 (216).

66 Martha C. Nussbaum, *Upheavals of Thought: The Intelligence of Emotions* (Cambridge: Cambridge University Press, 2001), 66.

67 Ibid. 1.

68 Oliver Davies, *A Theology of Compassion: Metaphysics of Difference and the Renewal of Tradition* (London: SCM Press, 2001), 56.

69 I am not suggesting that Nussbaum would disagree with Augustine in this regard, only that the emphasis is different.

5

Healing

Healing in the Christian world is multidimensional. The suffering it alleviates can be the longing for the eternal presence of the garden that we, as temporal beings, discern fleetingly in the rhythms of nature. As I have put it, "Who would have dreamed what those limbs withheld, as we survey the improbable street-lined trees in what we now call the off-season,/A beauty spared from prying eyes, waiting for shape to take hold of the thing and/Liberate its form from the night of anticipation, where sleep will give way to the hope of fullness." Just a glimpse of what is to come, this kind of longing can only be deferred and never resolved here. Suffering can also be the moral and spiritual degradation of being separated from God, or simply the discomfort and shame associated with physical decline. Amid such possibilities, healing involves the change from partiality into wholeness across some kind of temporal progression. Healing is said to have occurred when a lowly state of feeling, acting, or physical being transforms into what we, in our nature, perceive as a higher one.

Healing in Time

Augustine understood that emotional healing is connected to time, but inconsistently. In one sense, he knew that emotional wounds diminish over the course of time through the cooling effects of memory. In another sense, he lamented that the passage of time might soothe painful feelings without healing them fully. This was the case with respect to the sadness he had felt when his friend died. The reason for the incompleteness was that prior to situating himself in the presence of God he had experienced time as concrete and linear. One moment followed another with no particular commitment other than the sequence of events he felt bound by. With still no awareness of the salvific time of the divine economy, he saw time as a container of life's experiences and deeds traveling straight through the senses. Its capacity to heal was associated with the property of substitution, by which painful memories were replaced, one after another, with new hopes and different experiences.

After his conversion, time had the capacity to become intangible and circular, as we saw with respect to the moment of sublime understanding he shared with Monica in the garden. Christ's suffering, death, and resurrection had rendered time an infinite mystery that enveloped human experience in the steadfastness of faith. Shaped by the narrative of redemption, time became filled with the permanence of divine love. It did not heal according to the momentary substitution brought about by changing events. In this new paradigm, time circled backward and forward in the context of a divine love that overcame its linear constraints. Christ's Incarnation healed the past sin of Adam in order to heal the past, present, and future sins of humanity. The suffering Christ experienced in the Garden of Olives and then on the cross healed humanity's emotional wounds further by sharing in our suffering. The potential for human beings to heal over the course of time, morally and emotionally, was joined thoroughly with the paradox of Christ the Word, where divinity and mortal flesh united, so that "mortal flesh might not be forever mortal." This is where linear time meets salvific time to transform body and soul.

What Augustine shared with Monica in the garden was a longing for, and a glimpse of, the eternal truth of salvation. As temporal beings, they were altered briefly by the eternity of the Word, because they had been allowed to participate in the Word. The moment they relished together happened because each had professed faith in God's willingness and capacity to heal. Augustine would not have experienced such a moment while serving as an auditor among the Manichaeans, who had taught him that redemption separated the remnants of the cosmic light from the darkness of the world. That kind of salvation was a process of purification, rather than healing. Their christ was a morally superior and emotionally detached human being who shared neither in God's divinity nor in our human suffering. In the Manichaean paradigm, spiritual transformation involved the decontamination of the elite from the evil that was their accidental world.

The Therapy of the Word

With respect to Christ the Word, transformation involved a reordering of the human person according to the healing mechanism in the encounter with the truth of the Incarnation. Faith had taught Augustine that the singleness of the Word that became human flesh could heal the doubleness of our sinful flesh, such that Christ's "singleness corresponds with our doubleness."[1] We should note that the singleness of the Word has nothing to do with the Christological position articulated by certain opponents of the later Council of Chalcedon (451), namely that Christ consisted of only one nature, the divine. To the contrary, Augustine followed Ambrose in articulating the distinction of the human and divine natures of Christ without making them "strangers to one another."[2] His position was anti-Manichaean because it acknowledged the integrity of Christ's human nature as well as its thorough union with the divine, thereby making one single God-man Christ.

The singleness of Christ resided in his unique person, on the one hand, and in the harmony between his will and his moral actions, on the other. It was the singleness of these two aspects of Christ that healed what Augustine called "our doubleness," which is really just the difference between our longing for eternal truth and the reality of our fallen nature. We are double because we cannot become what we aspire to be without God's intervention. There is a tension in our nature, the result of our broken doubleness, that should not be confused with the paradox of the two-in-oneness of the God-man Christ.

Augustine is clear about the underlying mechanism that makes our doubleness congruous with Christ's singleness. It is related to the musical principle in which multiple voices join to form one harmonious chord. "I mean to say this coadaptation, as it occurs to me now, which the Greeks call 'harmony'."[3] When even one voice sings out of tune the melody becomes dissonant and out of synch with the principles of harmonic resonance. When each voice sings correctly, however, a consonant chord is formed, the beauty of which is obvious to all. The musical analogy is meant to illustrate that a certain consonance between doubleness and singleness has been implanted in us as part of our human nature. With respect to music, this consonance is apparent when each voice sings its melody to contribute to the harmonic integrity of the musical chord. With respect to salvation, this consonance falls into place when the human nature of Christ joins with us in what Augustine calls *coaptatio* or "coadaptation." The process unites two human natures, Christ's and ours, to produce one integral human being. It is the so-called "well-ordered monochord" that Augustine spoke of in the context of his musical analogy. Just as multiple tones contribute to the harmonic resonance of a single chord, two consonant natures come together to produce a newly perfected and harmonious human being. This harmony consists of replacing sin with righteousness and death with life. As Augustine put it, in becoming a perfectly righteous man, the Word Incarnate joined to us "the likeness of his humanity and took away the unlikeness of our unrighteousness, and by being made a participant in our mortality, God made us participants in God's divinity."[4]

This mutual participation with respect to God and human beings makes it possible for our temporal nature, with its love of temporal things, to be infused with eternal truth. In spite of the misguided love that carries us over to sin, Augustine believed that the longing for the presence of God and for God's eternal truth persists. "But eternal life is promised to us through the truth, from the clear knowledge of which, again, our faith stands as far apart as mortality does from eternity."[5] The longing for truth can be satisfied only by transforming our nature, first, according to the Christological principle of coadaptation already mentioned and, second, according to the ancient philosophical and medical principle "like heals like." In both cases, the transformation of our nature comes about because the Incarnation infuses that which needs to be healed in us with the same thing that spiritually degrades us. It is like a blood transfusion that cleanses us with a purer version of the contaminated thing that we already are. For Augustine, the cleansing that takes place as a result of the Incarnation permeates our temporal nature with the similar, though purified, temporality of Christ's human nature, such that we are healed by the very thing we were made sick by. "For health is the opposite of sickness, but the intermediate process of healing does not lead to health unless there is congruity with the sickness."[6]

There are limits, of course, to what this "congruity with sickness" includes, for not every temporal thing is the right sort of thing to heal our temporal nature. As Augustine put it, "Temporal things that are useless deceive the sick; temporal things that are useful sustain those that need healing and pass them on healed to eternal things."[7] The method by which the Incarnation heals is, for Augustine, similar to the remedies used in medical practice. It had long been established in the Hippocratic corpus that physicians were to alleviate symptoms by applying remedies consistent with the patient's constitution.[8] For example, those with a generally warm constitution who are made ill by cold might be relieved by the application of warmth, whereas those of a cold constitution who are made ill by heat might be relieved by the application of something cold. In such cases it was thought that unnatural change had produced illness that was then alleviated by applying the opposite of what had caused it. In other cases, however, the Hippocratic physician observed that patients were cured when he applied as a remedy the same stimulus that had induced the illness. For example, a small dose of a stomach irritant was found to cure an upset stomach. This is the medical principle that Augustine was alluding to when he spoke of the "congruity with sickness" that was necessary to bring about the desired cure.

Both types of remedies are relevant to Augustine's understanding of the Incarnation. Consistent with what we find in the Hippocratic corpus, Augustine was aware that healing takes place not only when "like" is applied to "like," as discussed above, but also when the remedy of opposites is applied. "Just as surgeons when they wrap wounds do not do so carelessly, but rather properly, so that there is even a certain degree of attractiveness in the binding in addition to its usefulness, so too our medicine of Wisdom was, by its assumption of humanity, adapted to our wounds, curing some by their opposites and some by what is similar."[9] The flexibility of the remedy is appropriate to the variable nature of wounds, some of which require the "opposite remedy" of cold compresses applied to hot wounds, while others require the "like remedy" of round bandages applied to round wounds. At times the remedy is so awful that it requires exceptional fortitude on the part of the patient. As Augustine preached to his congregation, for example, a diseased limb might have to be removed to avoid the inevitable "worms of infection."[10] In such a situation, the physician asked the patient to endure the pain of amputation in order to restore the wholeness of health. It was not a question simply of applying medical principles, such as "like heals like," but rather of finding the appropriate remedy, no matter how unpleasant, to treat the wound. The challenge was in getting people to recognize that healing involved not only the skill of the physician but also the effort and commitment of patients whose health depended on following the regimen the physician had devised for them.[11]

Physician for the Soul

Christ is the physician par excellence, the so-called *Christus medicus* who understands precisely the remedy needed to treat the particular moral and spiritual wound. In contrast with the physician who selects only the medicine necessary for the treatment, Christ is both the physician and the medicine. As the Wisdom of God, he is, at the same time *ipse medicus, ipsa medicina*. Because Christ himself is the cure—"the complete physician of our wounds"[12]—the remedy of his person is synonymous with the unfolding of the divine economy and its treatment of our spiritual degradation. Christ healed with the remedy of opposites, for example, when he healed our pride with his humility, when his mortality brought us to life, and when our vices were cured by his virtues. He healed with the remedy of likenesses when he was born of a woman to save us who fell through a woman, when "he came as a man to save us who are men, as a mortal to save us who are mortals, and by his death to save us who were dead."[13] The precise correspondence between such opposites and similarities upset normal reality by presenting all at once and out of sequence the ailment and the cure.

This is different from the secular time that Augustine had known and suffered through prior to his conversion. We have already seen how the young Augustine, by grieving death without the immortality of the Word, had moved through time as though it promised some conception of himself he feared and hoped would soon fade away. With respect to the sacred time of the divine economy, however, time moved back and forth indifferent to, and unbound by, the sequential experience of human suffering. The sin of the garden anticipated the remedy of Christ, who, in the light of that primal sin, healed in his person all aspects of our fallen nature through all points in time.

Christ's most fundamental mode of healing transcends even the atemporal precision with which his remedies healed humanity's transgressions. The fact of the Incarnation—that the majesty of the Word assumed the lowliness of our flesh—brings about the substance of the cure. "Because the word became flesh and dwelt among us, by his very nativity he made an eye-salve from which were cleansed the eyes of our heart, and we were then able to see his majesty through his humility."[14] The healing of the eyes that Augustine spoke of is multidimensional. First, it uses the principle of likeness: just as ours eyes had been closed with the dust from the earth and made unable to see the light, that same dust from the earth makes an eye-salve—a *collyrium*—to adapt our eyes to the glory of Christ. Second, it uses the eye-salve as a figure or image—known as a *typus* in the Latin—of the nativity. The typological imagery solidifies the connection between our sight and the truth of the Incarnation. Finally, Augustine argued from the curative principle of likeness and the combinative principle of typology that the Word became flesh both as a remedy for our spiritual wounds and as the truth that allows our eyes to see the paradox of the Word. "No one can see His glory unless he is healed by the humility of His flesh."[15]

The glory in humility of the Incarnation is the essential fullness of the new reality in Christ. For Augustine, this fullness consists in the faith and grace that we received when the Word became flesh. He reached this conclusion from his exegesis of John 1:16, which he rendered like this: "And from his fullness have we all received, and grace for grace."[16] From examining the Greek manuscripts he knew that the content of what precisely we received had been left unexpressed and that the clause that followed, i.e., "grace for grace," should be understood as an addendum to the main clause. What we received was, therefore, not only grace, he said, but also the faith that makes us favorable to God that we may be able to receive the unmerited gift of grace given to us in the Incarnation.[17] That the biblical text had left out the word "faith" perhaps underscored for Augustine that faith is, in the words of Hebrews 11:1, "the evidence of things unseen."[18]

For Augustine, the fundamental healing brought about by the Word is the ability to perceive the paradox of glory in humility that Christ's persecutors were unable to see.[19] This is the substance of the faith we were healed into when the eye-salve made from the earth cleansed the dust from our eyes. It is the truth of "His fullness that souls received, that they may be blessed" (John 1:16) and renewed by the wisdom that remains in them.[20] It is the paradox of humility coexisting with divinity, which was so self-evidently true for Augustine that he found a similar truth expressed in the books of the Platonists. "Jesus Christ, though he was in the form of God, did not regard equality with God something to be exploited, but emptied himself, taking the form of a slave, being born in human likeness, and being found in human form, he humbled himself and became obedient to the point of death, even death on a cross" (Phil. 2:6–8).[21]

The theological framework for apprehending this truth encompassed all of salvation history. Augustine understood that the deception that had taken place in the garden had dimmed our perception of a reality that was true and independent of our willingness to acknowledge it. The renewal of our vision with an eye-salve made of dust from the earth can be viewed in this context as a remedy for that primordial deception. The first step in our spiritual cleansing, it let us see the axiomatic truth that formed the substance of our cure. The sin of pride by which we had fallen was and is to be healed by the remedy of humility that Christ applied in order to save us. The repetition with which Augustine made this point has long been noted by commentators: "Again and again he tells his hearers that it was by the Divine Physician's humility that mankind was cured from the deadly tumor of pride, which had caused the fall of the first parents, and that, accordingly, the Redemption was nothing else but the neutralization of man's pride by God's humility."[22]

There is good reason for Augustine to have emphasized pride over all the other sins. Pride had deprived humanity of its self-understanding in relation to God and had brought it to its fallen state. Pride's inherent misperception had made Adam and Eve think they could disobey God without compromising their bliss. Pride had even prevented the pagan philosophers from fulfilling the truth they claimed to serve. As Augustine said of the Platonist Porphyry in *City of God*: if you had really loved virtue and wisdom you would have come to know Christ as the virtue and wisdom of God, "instead of being so inflated with pride in your empty knowledge that you recoiled from His most healthful humility."[23] In response to a young scholar, Dioscorus, who had wished to study pagan literature and philosophy, Augustine remarked that we hold onto truth in three ways: "the first is humility, the second is humility, and the third is humility, and this I would say as often as you ask, not that there are no other directions that may be given, but because unless humility precedes, accompanies, and follows every good action that we do...pride wrenches it all at once from our hand."[24] Augustine had seen in Dioscorus the duplicity that was the hallmark of pride. Although he had claimed to seek knowledge and truth, he had wanted simply to secure a good reputation among men. To look for the supreme truth in anything other than God, said Augustine, would be like seeking a cure to a life-threatening ailment in fine food and clothing instead of in medicine and physicians.[25]

The good physician did more than calculate the remedy needed to bring about a cure. Healing also took place in the context of the physician–patient relationship. Augustine alluded to this relational aspect of healing when he talked about the psychological strategy the physician used when dealing with a patient who was averse to treatment. "'Drink it,' he says, 'drink it, in order to live.' And so the sick man may not reply, 'I can't, I won't do it, I will not drink it,' the physician, though he is healthy, drinks first, so the sick man won't hesitate to drink it."[26] Embedded in this strategy is the sense that the physician heals our ailments by bringing his health to bear upon our illness.

The connection between the sickness of the patient and the wholeness of the physician was there in the medical tradition long before Augustine. With respect to the potential burdens of such a connection, Hippocrates had lamented famously that the physician gathered sorrows of his own from others' misfortunes. The observation was as much an approval of the phenomenon of shared grief as it was an admonition of the emotional fatigue the physician might have to face in the light of so much suffering. Regrettably, Hippocrates was silent regarding the precise mechanism by which this emotional contagion took place.

What we do know is that Hippocratic medicine understood the human body as a composite of four constituent elements: blood, phlegm, yellow bile, and black bile. This was in contrast to certain philosophers and physicians who had claimed that the body was a unity consisting, for example, only of blood, or only of bile. The Hippocratic corpus rejected such a view on two grounds: first, that human reproduction would not have been possible if the body were composed of a single, undifferentiated element;[27] and, second, that human beings would not experience either change and corruption or excess and deficiency[28] and, therefore, would not have to endure the suffering that we recognize as pain.[29] The latter objection assumed that multiplicity was necessary in order for the body to undergo change and to experience any sort of degradation of its normal functioning. Pain was understood among Hippocratic physicians as the result of an imbalance among the body's constituent elements. As Hippocrates put it, "One feels pain whenever one of these elements is lesser or greater, or is isolated in the body and is not compounded with the others."[30] The pain of elemental imbalance or isolation occurs, for example, when blood, bile, or phlegm leaves one part of the body inappropriately and enters another. Health, in contrast, results from the correct proportion of elements with respect to mixture, capacity, and magnitude. One can speculate that the Hippocratic physiology of human suffering allowed for the possibility that physical bodies relate to one another through the correspondence of the same primary elements from which they are composed.[31]

Prior to Augustine, the Hippocratic sentiment noted above—that "the physician gathers sorrows of his own from others' misfortunes"—had been amplified among such theologians as Gregory Nazianzen and Eusebius. Upon the death of Gregory's brother, Caesarius, a physician, Gregory had consoled family and friends with the observation that Caesarius would no longer be burdened with illnesses or made to suffer grief as a result of others' misfortunes.[32] The oration Gregory delivered on the occasion of his brother's funeral was itself an invitation for those experiencing a similar loss to join in the mourning. They were supposed to share in his grief and "learn to feel the pain" of other people's suffering.[33] Several points are worth highlighting: first, that the physician was presumed to experience grief in the course of his duties; second, that a shared encounter with grief was thought to be emotionally healing; and finally, that among the general population, sensing someone else's pain was a skill that could be—and, apparently, should be—learned.

In the early fourth century, Eusebius of Caesarea had already interpreted this same Hippocratic "physician of sorrows" in a Christian context. Whereas Gregory would later use the concept to impart a practical moral lesson, Eusebius was committed to unearthing its Christological implications. For Eusebius, Christ was the excellent physician who put on our corrupted and mortal nature to perceive our miseries, to touch our wounds, and to derive his pain from the misfortunes of others.[34] Like the physician that healed our bodies while compassionately feeling our pain, Christ healed the same broken nature that he experienced when the Word became flesh.

Salvation was understood in this context as an emotional form of healing based on the philosophical principle "like heals like." It should be distinguished from the model of substitutionary atonement articulated, for instance, in Matthew 20:28, in which Christ saved humanity from sin and death by giving his own life as a sacrifice. It can be distinguished as well from the model of recapitulative atonement, in which salvation takes place, as in 1 Corinthians 15:45, through the repetition and correction of key events in economic history, such as the Fall, that led to our corruption. Of the two, Christ's compassionate healing of our mortal wounds has more in common with recapitulative atonement, which links all aspects of our fallen nature with the human, though perfected, nature of Christ in his single divine-human person. This is how Christ healed our pride with his humility and how his immortality healed our mortal flesh. I have already remarked that this recapitulative approach to our salvation healed by the remedy of opposites in a typological reconstruction of time according to the principles of renewal and transformation. The model of emotional atonement healed by the remedy of likeness.

The Gospel accounts of Jesus' ministry are the basis for the *Christus medicus* theme. From Mark 2:17 we learn, for example, that Jesus said, "The strong have no need of a physician, but the sick. I have come not to call the righteous, but sinners."[35] The Gospel accounts are also the basis for our understanding that Jesus' healings and miracles were emotionally charged. Mark 8:2 reports that Jesus felt compassion before he fed the crowd of 4,000 with loaves and fish; likewise, when Jesus healed the leper who approached him asking to be cleansed (Mark 1:40–1), when he healed the sick among the crowds that followed him (Mt. 14:14),

when he was surrounded by a distressed and wearied crowd
(Mt. 9:36; Mark 6:34), and when he raised a widow's only son from
the dead (Lk. 7:12–13). In all cases, the Gospels use the Greek word
splanchnon and its derivatives to refer to the intense sympathy that
Jesus felt toward the suffering he witnessed.[36] Jesus did not merely
heal the sick, the lame, the blind, the demonically possessed, and
the downtrodden. He felt the same pain of isolation, sorrow, and
social dislocation as the people he came into contact with. As Henri
Nouwen put it, "They moved him, they made him feel with all his
intimate sensibilities the depth of their sorrow. He became lost with
the lost, hungry with the hungry, and sick with the sick. In him, all
suffering was sensed with a perfect sensitivity."[37]

In its original meaning, the word *splanchnon* referred to the guts
and entrails. Specifically, it signified the organs, "the heart, lungs,
liver, kidneys, which in sacrifices were reserved to be eaten by the
sacrificers at the beginning of their feast."[38] It was used in this literal
sense, for example, in the *Agamemnon* of Aeschylus to describe
the grotesque slaughter of Thyestes' children.[39] It is worth noting
that the later usage is already foreshadowed here in the context
of horror: next to the graphic use of the word *splanchnon* to refer
to the children's entrails, the word *epoikistos*, meaning "pitiful," is
used to evoke the burden of the loss that Thyestes endured.

The transformation of *splanchnon* from something horrific
into something compassionate occurred when the connection was
drawn between the organs as merely the flesh and blood that keep
us alive and as the metaphorical and physical seat of our emotions.
This latter usage is present already, for instance, in Exodus 2:6 to
describe the benevolent disposition of the Pharaoh's daughter upon
rescuing Moses along the banks of the Nile. In approximately the
second century CE, the *Testament of Levi* used the word to evoke
God's tender mercy.[40] Likewise, the *Testament of Zebulun* used it
to describe the feeling Zebulun felt upon seeing a man naked in the
wintertime, as well as the action he took—he removed a garment
from his father's house—to alleviate the man's distress.

In Origen, we find the two images drawn together, the physician
as a dispenser of remedies in the Hippocratic tradition and
the physician as a kind-hearted healer of the sick. Jesus is the
"benevolent physician who looks for those who are sick that he
may offer them remedies and heal them."[41] Similarly for Augustine,
Jesus is the ultimate physician whose diagnostic skill never failed,

whose generosity required no compensation, and whose remedies applied to every conceivable ailment.[42] Absent, though, is the explicit development of the "benevolent physician" type of the *Christus medicus* theme into what one might call the "compassionate physician." It is articulated thoroughly in the sixth century, by which time the image of the physician as a compassionate healer had taken hold of the Christian imagination. Gary Ferngren has shown that Cassiodorus (d. *c.585*), the Roman statesman and scholar who founded a monastery at Vivarium in southern Italy, commended his monks who were also physicians for being "sad at the suffering of others, sorrowful for those who are in danger, grieved at the pain of those who are received, and always distressed with personal sorrow at the misfortunes of others."[43] The feeling of compassion for human suffering was supposed to be joined with the utmost skill in the properties of herbs and the compounding of drugs. At the same time, the physician-monk was never to lose sight of the fact that the ultimate healer was Jesus, in whose name he practiced the art of medicine.

When Jesus brought compassion to bear upon our suffering he was acting as more than just a sympathetic physician. For Augustine, the image of the *Christus medicus* evoked the skillful precision with which Christ applied each and every remedy appropriate to our cure. Yet there were limits to what a physician could do. The metaphor of the "good physician"—even the Hippocratic "physician of sorrows"—could account for neither the intensity nor the effectiveness of the shared emotion by which Christ healed spiritual wounds. It was associated too closely with ordinary medical cures to illuminate the multilayered transformation that happens in Christ.

The Emotions of Christ

Augustine understood that healing takes place through the unique person of Christ and not solely through the human nature that Christ assumed. The Manichaeans had undermined this personal unity, according to Augustine, by separating the suffering Christ "whom the earth conceives and brings forth by the power of the Holy Spirit," from the Christ who was crucified under Pontius

Pilate, and from the Christ who, as the virtue and wisdom of God, dwells in the sun and the moon.[44] As a point of comparison, the further weakening of the connection between God and Jesus can be seen in the Coptic *Kephalaia*, which described Jesus' descent into matter as a drawn-out process of purification. Having boarded ten vehicles to journey through certain key points and moral concepts that are necessary for redemption, Jesus manifests in the flesh to make alive, redeem, and give victory to those who are his.[45] Rather an agent of God than God in the flesh, the Coptic Manichaean Jesus is an excellent man who carries out "the pleasure of his Father."[46] This view of Jesus and of Christ was apparently based on the notion of a moral union with God that was used to bring about spiritual redemption.

This was the root of the problem. The distinction the Manichaeans had drawn between the son of God and the Son of man, and among the various manifestations of Christ, undercut the unity of his person to the point that our suffering could not have been healed. Such a moral union was insufficient for redemption because it did not align human nature with God. It brought our spiritual corruption simply into contact with an elevated man. As Augustine said in a different context, "the believer, I say, who in Him believes and confesses the true human nature that is ours, however much it was singularly elevated by its assumption by God the Word into the only Son of God, so that He who assumed, and what He assumed, should be one person in Trinity."[47] Not only was the unity of subject that Augustine described far greater than a moral union, it was also more than the union of two natures. In going so much deeper than that, the unity he articulated addressed both the Christological anomaly of two separate divine and human natures that certain Christians from Antioch had proposed and the so-called separation of the son of God from the Son of man articulated by some among the Manichaeans. Both kinds of multiplicity threatened the truth that Christ is neither the Word alone, nor the flesh alone, but the Word made flesh.[48] Tarsicius J. van Bavel has shown, for instance, that Augustine's thought evolved after 400 CE to the extent that the hypostatic union of the human and divine natures in Christ was seen as an action of the Incarnate Word, which was said to have assumed, received, taken, joined, and adapted human nature in the unity of the person.[49]

Emotions are the most profound aspect of human nature that the Word assumed. We have seen in Chapter 3 how Augustine came to appreciate over time that affective engagement with human suffering was necessary for virtue to flourish. Certain pagan philosophers, such as some among the Stoics, had subscribed to an ideal that insisted on their avoiding other people's emotional pain. Shared suffering was thought to compromise the emotional tranquility that the wise man strived for. Yet Augustine knew otherwise from both the ethic of charity recorded in Scripture and the philosophical reflections of Cicero. We are told in *City of God* that he, like Cicero, had determined that the philosophical disagreements among the pagans with respect to the purpose of our affective life had been superficial. Compassion for human misery was supposed to override any such misguided pursuit of emotional tranquility. This universal truth emerged when Augustine made pagan philosophy into a unified moral psychology. He was saying that even the pagans had understood, beneath their endless quarrels, that affective compassion was virtuous. The insight confirmed the universality of compassion as a virtue everyone should subscribe to. At the same time, it undercut the charge made by pagan intellectuals that a distinctly Christian ethic of compassion had so weakened the collective resolve of the commonwealth that Rome had become vulnerable to the Visigoths.

The emotional life of Christ can be illuminated in the context of the universal truth that emerges from this apologetic agenda. As Augustine put it in *City of God* 14.9,

> But since these emotions [that derive from charity] are the result of *correct reasoning* (*recta ratio*) when they are used in a way that is appropriate, who would then dare to call them diseases or morbid passions? So too, when the Lord himself condescended to lead a human life in the form of a slave, yet remaining wholly free from sin, he used these emotions where he judged that they ought to be used. (emph. suppl)[50]

Once Augustine realized that feeling emotion for other people's suffering was the moral consequence of our "correct reasoning," he could then conclude that there was nothing wrong inherently with our affective life. In the light of this moral psychological insight, it was only natural for him to find that Christ had experienced such emotions.

Augustine fleshed this out in several ways. First, the human emotions in Christ were genuine. He was at times angry, glad, and grieved, as the Scriptures indicated. Second, Christ made use of our emotions, as Augustine put it, when Christ determined that they should be made use of. To make this argument, Augustine chose the Latin verb "*adhibeo*," meaning "to use" or "to apply," rather than any number of verbs he could have chosen, meaning "to feel." The linguistic decision highlighted the Christological point that it was Christ who decided if and when it was appropriate for him to assume our emotional state. From this it follows, for Augustine, that Christ "assumed these emotions in his human mind for the sake of the settled dispensation when he wished to do so, just as he had become a man when he wished to do so."[51] Unlike our experience of such virtuous emotions as charity and compassion, which we sometimes feel even when we prefer not to, Christ's emotions were entirely under his control. He was never the subject of unwanted emotional fluctuation.

Related to this is the third point that Christ's lack of emotional necessity heightened his experience of our suffering. Augustine made this clear when he reflected upon Christ's agony in the Garden of Olives. As the Lord considered his looming passion, he could have chosen to be free from sadness. That he did not do so is a testament to the strength that the Lord exhibited in the context of human weakness. "Was he not bearing your weakness, when he said, 'Sad is my soul even unto death'? Matthew 26:38 Was he not figuring yourself in himself, when he was saying, 'Father, if it be possible, let this cup pass from me?' Matthew 26:39."[52] The decision he made to feel what humanity feels is an act of compassion he carried out in strength. What made it compassionate is the fact that his feelings were the result of a voluntary decision to feel them. "Thus when the Only-Begotten himself, bearing your weakness and prefiguring your person in himself—just as the head assumes the person of its own body—drew near to his passion he was sorrowful by reason of the human nature he bore in order to gladden you; he was sorrowful in order to comfort you."[53] Notice that, for Augustine, the reason for Christ's sorrow is "the human nature he bore," that it is the "Only-Begotten himself"—not simply his human nature—that endured our weakness, and that his sorrow is the source of our comfort.

Christ made our sadness his without compromising the integrity of the feeling. Although the sadness he experienced is ours, it is not a virtual sadness. The sadness is real because it is felt compassionately on our behalf. Recall that Augustine said in *City of God*, "What is compassion but a kind of sympathy in our heart for the suffering of another that surely compels us to help as much as we can?"[54] We have already seen that Augustine quarreled with certain of the pagan philosophers for their unwillingness to acknowledge other-regarding emotions as potentially virtuous. For Augustine, there is no sense in which a feeling that originates in other people's sorrows is any less real than a feeling that originates in our own. In fact, after his reworking of pagan philosophy, such charitable emotions become the moral and spiritual norm. The difference, for Augustine, between Christ's affections and ours is that ours derive from the necessity of our human nature and from the conflict between our passions and our will because of the Fall. Christ's are entirely voluntary and are never in conflict. It is possible to say that Christ truly felt—and continues to feel—the human emotion of sadness to the extent that he compassionately embraced our condition. To put it simply, whereas our emotions were tarnished by the Fall, Christ's were and always will be the perfect expression of the other-regarding emotions Augustine identified as being necessary for the virtuous life: "We have these [feelings] from the weakness of the human condition; but it was not so with the Lord Jesus, whose weakness came from power" (*City of God* 14.9). Christ's emotions are real because they are felt compassionately on our behalf.

Augustine deepened our understanding of the relationship among the body of Christ that suffers, the Christ who suffered on our behalf, and the God who healed us in the context of Christ's feeling of abandonment on the cross. "God, my God, why have you forsaken me?" said Jesus, in the words of Psalm 22. Augustine suggests that the abandonment was felt by the Word, through the human nature of Christ, and by the church, with Christ as its Head.[55] The mystery of this abandonment is the mystery of the relationship among Christ, humanity, and God as it plays out at the intersection of ecclesiology (the body of Christ, as in the church) and the Trinity (the three persons acting and abiding in one, single essence). With respect to ecclesiology, the cry of abandonment—"God, my God, why have you forsaken me?"—signals the cry of the mystical body of Christ in the light of our collective suffering. With respect to the Trinity, the interpretation is a negative one: the cry could not have been taken as true literally without compromising the essential oneness of the three persons of the Trinity. There is no ontological sense in which God could have abandoned Christ.

Aligning Human Emotions with God

For Augustine, the words of the Psalms, by the very act of their spiritual utterance, restructure the person uttering them into a new association with God. As Rowan Williams has observed, "The psalmist's voice is what releases two fundamentally significant things for the Augustinian believer. It unseals deep places, emotions otherwise buried, and it provides an analogy for the unity or intelligibility of a human life lived in faith."[56] "More than simply a 'devotional' reading of a holy text,"[57] the Psalms unearth emotions we did not know we had and transform them into the new story of a life lived in the context of God. For Augustine, this unearthing has to do with bringing what we suffer from in line with what we love, as we shall see below. By internalizing the Psalms according to the example he has set, for instance in the *Confessions*, they provide us with a kind of emotional excavation.

The specific emotion that Psalm 22 has unearthed is the feeling of spiritual abandonment, the fear of being removed—in some as yet unspecified way—from the presence of God. We have already seen that the most obvious interpretation, that of being separated ontologically from God, has to be rejected. For Augustine, the key to its interpretation is, rather, in the words of the psalm itself. The reason Christ felt abandoned on the cross was, as it says in Psalm 22.3, "Not that I may lack wisdom."[58] We are to take this to mean that Christ felt the feeling of abandonment so that he, in his body and in his church, and we, as the "least ones" that make up that church, may not lack the wisdom that "When you did it to one of my least ones, you did it to me" (Mt. 25:40).[59] In the light of this truth, the cry of abandonment on the cross cannot be the cry of spiritual isolation. It is a compassionate cry that links Christ as head with the body of Christ, which is the church of his believers. In such an intimate relationship, it is impossible to be removed from the presence of God.

Through an apparently simple rendering of the biblical text, Augustine has revealed a deep theological truth. By joining the cry of abandonment from Psalm 22 with additional words from the psalm, and then linking those words with similar passages from the Gospels, Augustine has "unsealed" for us the multilayered mystery of the relationship between God and human beings. From the example of Christ's cry of abandonment on the cross, we are supposed to conclude that happiness in a world such as this, which is inclined to love and cling to the wrong sorts of temporal things, should never prevail over the eternal good of salvation. The cry is not, therefore, the cry of desertion. It is the cry of our collective suffering, which has been exemplified for us in Christ as a call to prioritize eternal truth over temporal satisfaction. When we prioritize correctly, then what we suffer from becomes the emotional cry that brings us into greater alignment with what we love. The "emotional excavation" exposes and, therefore, neutralizes the fear of spiritual desolation in the light of suffering, so that, in the words of Rowan Williams, "when we hear Christ speaking 'our' words of anguish, we know that this cannot be so."[60]

The Physical Aspect

The diminution of the miraculous is another way to ensure that we do not come to value our physical comfort in this life over our soul's salvation in the next. In his early years Augustine believed that our existential suffering was no longer being miraculously healed. There was a difference between the plentiful miracles of apostolic times and their absence in our own, which he ascribed to a kind of God-imposed discipline. We were not to become too familiar with and, therefore, dependent upon the miraculous as a confirmation of the faith.[61] The fear was that continuously feeding our faith with miracles would make us grow cold and complacent. What had been a wonder for us to marvel at might become, with too frequent repetition, commonplace and familiar.

This view began to shift as stories of miraculous healings were brought to Augustine's attention, such as those his close friend Nebridius told about the miracles of the Egyptian hermit Antony. Augustine had been surprised to learn that such wonders had taken place so recently.[62] Likewise, we learn in the *Confessions* that the uncorrupted bodies of the martyrs Gervasius and Protasius had been discovered through a vision and then dug up and translated to Ambrose's church in Milan, where they were used to cast out unclean spirits and heal a blind man.[63] The event that finally changed Augustine's mind happened approximately three decades later in *c.*415 when the relics of St. Stephen, the martyr, were discovered and placed in numerous reliquaries. The widow, Galla, and her daughter, the consecrated virgin Simplicia, carried one such shrine to Augustine's church in Hippo.[64] The relics soon became a source of miraculous healing, the details of which he shared in the final book of *City of God* and preached about in several sermons.

One of the most conspicuous healings occurred around Easter in 424 involving a brother and sister, Paulus and Palladia, who were suffering from an uncontrollable trembling. From a noble family in Cappadocian Caesarea, they, along with their five brothers and sisters, had been cursed by their recently widowed mother for some wrong she believed they had committed against her. For the two weeks leading up to Easter, Paulus and Palladia attended church every day and prayed before the relics of St. Stephen for a cure. On Easter morning, before a large crowd of spectators, Paulus touched the bars of the reliquary and prayed. As he was praying, he passed out on the floor, though he was no longer trembling. When he regained consciousness, it was apparent to all who were present that he had been healed of his mother's curse. Three days later, Augustine asked Paulus, now healed, and Palladia, still trembling, to stand as he read and commented upon their story before the people. When he was finished, Palladia went of her own accord to the reliquary, touched its bars, and, like her brother, was healed miraculously. The people rejoiced that both she and her brother had been cured. "What was in the hearts of these exultant people but the faith of Christ, for which the blood of Stephen was shed?"[65]

This and other healings that had taken place at St. Stephen's shrine convinced Augustine that the miraculous, though not as glorious as in the past, had continued indeed into his own day. His church at Hippo was a case in point. When Augustine saw that the miracles happening there were similar to the divine powers that had thrived in the past he decided to chronicle them. The failure to report such events had contributed to the misperception that the miraculous had diminished greatly after the apostolic period.

These current miracles are scarcely known even to the whole population in the midst of which they are performed, and at best are confined to one location. For frequently they are known only to a very few persons, while the rest are ignorant of them, especially if the citizenry is large; and when they are reported to other people elsewhere, no such authority confirms them, that they may be believed without difficulty or doubt, although they are reported to and by faithful Christians.[66]

Augustine remedied the situation by creating a public register of miracles for Hippo. Within two years of the relics being moved there, close to seventy miracles had already been recorded, while the many others that occurred were likely remembered and passed around orally. Other towns could boast an even greater reputation for miraculous healings. Augustine attributed the large number of miracles documented in the nearby town of Calama, for instance, to the fact that the relics had been there longer and its miracles had been written down consistently for public consumption.[67]

The miracles Augustine witnessed and heard about in his own time persuaded him to interpret such events as a continuation of the signs and wonders of the past. Though they now occurred in a lesser form, they were not to be seen as isolated anomalies of divine power breaking through mundane experience. The same reasoning that had applied to our reception of the miraculous in the time of Cicero and of the emperors Augustus and Tiberius—a time Augustine described as enlightened and rational—also applied here. In such a time of reason, the resurrection of Christ's body and its ascension into heaven would not have been believed, he argued, were it not for the corroborating signs, and subsequent testimonies, that both events had happened.[68] We are meant to conclude that the rational mindset of Augustine's time insisted likewise upon a record of well-attested miracles to confirm the truth of what was being claimed. Two years after he concluded *City of God*, he was moved to revise earlier statements he had made with respect to miracles:

But what I said is not to be so interpreted that no miracles are believed to be performed in the name of Christ in the present time. For, when I wrote that book [i.e., *On the True Religion*], I myself had recently learned that a blind man had been restored to sight in Milan near the bodies of the martyrs in that very city, and I knew about some others, so numerous even in these times, that we cannot know about all of them nor enumerate those we know.[69]

Such instances of the miraculous were not just stories that circulated among a superstitious population. To the extent that they had been both witnessed and recorded in Augustine's time as in the past, healings such as these confirmed the divine power of Christ's Incarnation, death, and resurrection in an age that Augustine believed was an age of reason. As Serge Lancel has put it, "So a miracle was not an erratic phenomenon that eluded all rationality. For Augustine it had a firm theological foundation. But its impact on men's hearts was still as strong, for by this emergence from the natural order which was the only one they knew, God burst in upon them."[70]

The continuation of the miraculous, where God bursts onto our scene, confirms that mundane time, the busy distraction we live in, is still being punctuated with moments in which time is suspended. This is the soul being stretched and extended into the timeless present we yearn for. To acknowledge in stories and in public records that miracles are breaking through time is to corroborate the ongoing presence of divine power. Such interruptions of our temporal lives offer a momentary stillness from the longing for something we know we cannot have and that we look for in places it cannot be. For Augustine, the healing of our physical body and our fallen nature resolves this longing into wholeness.

Notes

1   August., *De Trin.*, 4.2.4.
2   The phrase is from Tarsicius J. van Bavel, *Recherches sur la Christologie de Saint Augustin. L'humain et le divin dans le Christ d'après Saint Augustin* (Fribourg: University Press of Fribourg, 1954), 26.
3   August., *De Trin.*, 4.2.4; see trans. Rev. Arthur West Haddan, *St. Augustin: On the Trinity*. NPNF 3 (Edinburgh: T&T Clark, repr. 1993), 71.
4   Ibid; see trans. Haddan, *On the Trinity*, 71.
5   Ibid. 4.18.24; 81.
6   Ibid.

7   Ibid.
8   Hippoc., *Loc. hom.* 42.
9   August., *De doct. Christ.*, 1.14; See trans. Rev. J. F. Shaw,
    On Christian Doctrine. NPNF 2 (Edinburgh: T&T Clark,
    repr. 1993), 526.
10 August., *Serm.*, 278, PL 38,1270, line 32.
11 See August., *Serm.*, 278.
12 August., *In Evang. Iohan.*, 3.3, line 5; trans. Rev. John Gibb, *St.
    Augustin: Lectures or Tractates on the Gospel According to St. John.*
    NPNF 7 (Edinburgh: T&T Clark, repr. 1991), 19.
13 August., *De doct. Christ.*, 1.14; see trans. Shaw, *On Christian
    Doctrine*, 526.
14 August., *In Evang. Iohan.*, 2.16, lines 1–2; trans. Gibb, *Gospel
    According to John*, 18.
15 Ibid. line 6; trans. Gibb, *Gospel According to John*, 18.
16 Ibid. 3.8, lines 1–2; see trans. Gibb, *Gospel According to John*, 21.
17 Ibid. 3.9, line 1.
18 My allusion to Heb. 11:1.
19 August., *In Evang. Iohan.*, 3.3.
20 August., *Conf.*, 7.9.14, citing Jn 1:16 in the context of Phil. 2:6–11.
21 As Augustine notes in *Conf.*, 7.9.14; see trans. J. G. Pilkington,
    The Confessions of St. Augustin. NPNF 1 (Edinburgh: T&T Clark,
    repr. 1994), 108.
22 Rudolph Arbesmann, O. S. A., "The Concept of 'Christus Medicus'
    in St. Augustine," *Traditio* 10 (1954): 1–28 (9).
23 August., *De civ. D.*, 10.28; trans. Wiesen, *The City of God*, 379.
24 August., *Ep.*, 118.3.22, cited by Arbesmann, "The Concept of
    'Christus Medicus'," 10; see also trans. Cunningham, *Letters of St.
    Augustine*, 446.
25 August., *Ep.*, 118.3.13.
26 August., *Serm.*, 88.7; trans. Edmund Hill, *The Works of Saint
    Augustine: Sermons*, 3/3 (New York: New City Press, 1991),
    423–424.
27 Hippoc., *De nat. hom.*, 3–4.
28 Hippoc., *Loc. hom.*, 42.
29 Hippoc., *De nat. hom.*, 2.
30 Ibid. 4.
31 Although Galen does not address this point specifically, see his
    commentary on Hippoc., *De nat. hom.*, 51–3, regarding the
    universal elements from which everything, including mankind, is
    made.
32 Gregory Naz., *Or.*, 7.20.
33 Ibid. 7.1.

34 Eusebius, *Hist. eccl.*, 10.4.11.
35 See parallels, Mt. 9:12–13 and Lk. 5:31–32.
36 Henri J. M. Nouwen, Donald P. McNeill, and Douglas A. Morrison, *Compassion: A Reflection on the Christian Life* (New York and London: Doubleday, 1982), 16–17.
37 Ibid. 17.
38 H. G. Liddell, R. Scott, and H. S. Jones, *Greek-English Lexicon. With a Revised Supplement* (Oxford: Clarendon Press, 1996), s.v., "splanchnon."
39 Aesch., *Ag.*, line 1221.
40 *Test. Lev.*, 4.4.
41 Origen, *C. Cels.*, 3.74.
42 August., *Serm.*, 386.3.2; *Serm.*, 175.8; *En. in Ps.*, 45.11, cited in Arbesmann, "The Concept of 'Christus Medicus'," 19–20.
43 Text and translation from Ferngren, *Medicine and Health Care*, 111.
44 August., *C. Faust. Man.*, 20.2; trans. Gardner and Lieu, *Manichaean Texts*, 219.
45 See ibid. 218, *Kephalaion* 8.
46 Ibid.
47 August., regarding the Pelagian controversy, in *De don. persev.*, 24, 67; see trans. Peter Holmes and Rev. Benjamin B. Warfield, *Saint Augustin: Anti-Pelagian Writings*. NPNF 5 (Edinburgh: T&T Clark, repr. 1991), 552.
48 See van Bavel, *Recherches sur la Christologie de Saint Augustin*, 23.
49 Ibid. 21.
50 August., *De civ. D.*, 14.9; see trans. Levine, *The City of God*, 311.
51 Ibid; see trans. Levine, *The City of God*, 311.
52 August., *En. in Ps.*, (65) 64.16; see Augustine, *Expositions on the Book of Psalms* (Veritatis Splendor Publications, repr. 2012).
53 August., *En. in Ps.*, (32) 31.26 (2).
54 August., *De civ. D.*, 9.5.
55 August., *Ep.*, 140.11.28.
56 Williams, *On Augustine*, 26.
57 Ibid.
58 In the Latin Bible that Augustine used it is Ps. 21.3 (22).
59 August., *Ep.*, 140.11.28.
60 Williams, *On Augustine*, 28.
61 August., *De ver. rel.*, 25.47.
62 August., *Conf.*, 8.6.
63 August., *Conf.*, 9.7.
64 August., *Ep.*, 212.

65 August., *De civ. D.*, 22.8, line 480; trans. Marcus Dods, "The City of God," in ed. Philip Schaff, *Nicene and Post-Nicene Fathers* (Edinburgh: T&T Clark, repr. 1993), 491.
66 Ibid. lines 29–33; trans. Dods, *The City of God*, 485.
67 Ibid. 22.8.
68 Ibid. 22.7.
69 August., *Retract.*, 12.7, revising *De ver. rel.*, 25.47; trans. Sister Mary Inez Bogan, *Saint Augustine: The Retractations*. The Fathers of the Church 60 (Washington, DC: The Catholic University of America Press, 1968), 55.
70 Lancel, *St. Augustine*, 468.

6

Accommodation

Truth for Augustine is absolute. It cannot be negotiated, subdued, or managed. It lingers in memory even when we do not have the courage to admit its presence. He knew that in this fallen world our relationship to truth is ambivalent. There scarcely is a person alive who would not acknowledge his or her commitment to its existence and to the benefits of a truthful life. There seemingly is no end to the ways in which our relationship to truth can be, and often is, subverted to our desire to conform to the mechanisms of the world. When this happens, truth still persists as an ideal. It continues to be held up as a thing to admire and strive for, even while its principles no longer shape the lives—and by extension, the societies—of those who claim such principles for themselves.

Spiritual Fulfillment

Truth for Augustine consisted in the blessed and happy life. Not long after he rejected Manichaeism for failing to unveil the truth he was seeking, he retired from public life as the leading rhetorician in Milan to a quiet country estate in Cassiciacum, where he pursued what he would later call "a Christian life" among like-minded friends. Together they pondered the meaning of truth and the extent, and manner in which, we acquire it. They understood this to be wisdom, which they defined as the search for, and knowledge of, things human and divine that are consistent with happiness.[1] It remained for them to define what precisely they meant when they spoke of happiness as the common goal of human beings. Quite simply, they argued, happiness consists in having what one wants, and to the extent that all want truth, it consists not in pursuing, but in discovering truth as something that can be held onto and counted upon for its stability.[2]

The argument was meant to defeat the skepticism of the Academics, a philosophical school that found an odd sort of comfort in searching for truth but never really getting it.[3] As Blake D. Dutton put it,

> Augustine was unimpressed with the Socratic ideal of the good life. This was the ideal of a life dedicated to inquiry that leads to wisdom, not as expert knowledge of practical or speculative matters, but rather as awareness of ignorance. In the case of the Academics, such wisdom manifests itself, not only in disavowals of knowledge, but also in acts of withholding assent.[4]

The Academics were unwilling to assert that anything apart from their philosophical method of inquiry was true. Their commitment to epistemological uncertainty meant that they never would be wrong. Later, Augustine would argue with the Pelagians for a similar kind of pride in the possibility of human self-sufficiency as a means of circumventing God, as we shall see.

For Augustine, the greatest part of happiness, and therefore of truth, comes in recognizing that we are an image of God. On the basis of this truth he asserted, "we both are and know that we are, and we love that we are and that we know this."[5] Augustine could make such a claim, against the skepticism of the Academics, because it was grounded in the truth of our nature. "Just as I know that I am, so too I also know this, that I know,"[6] that is to say, the knowledge of his existence as a real and substantial thing could not be washed away in short-lived illusions, neither in those of the Manichaeans nor of the skeptics. He knew that our existence is real, not real in the sense that God is real, but in the sense that it is true, and when it is loved as true, then "the love itself is also true and certain."[7] For Augustine, the reality of our existence as an image of the triune God is the foundation of our happiness: "for how can a person be happy if he is nothing?"[8] With the true knowledge of our being, we are able then to live the happy life, not just by living according to our mind and reason (as he said at Cassiciacum prior to his conversion),[9] but by living according to God (as he later said in his *Retractations*).[10]

Unhappiness is the result of a self-deception that permeates our fallen nature. It can be traced to the primal deception committed by the serpent who, in his cleverness, enticed Eve to disobey God.[11] Running through our veins, self-deception resists admitting that the self has been deceived. It desires its commitment to truth to the extent that it cannot imagine that what it desires, as if it were true, is not, in fact, so. The deception, according to Augustine, consists in the universal love for truth, which often longs for whatever truth it may desire, and then in the subsequent reluctance to accept that we, in the choices we have made and in the things we have longed for, have been deceived.

Its logical conclusion is the paradox of unhappiness that has unfolded in the name of truth: "They therefore hate the truth because of that thing that they love instead of truth. They love truth when it enlightens them, but they hate it when it refutes them. Because they would not willingly be deceived and do not wish to deceive, they love it when it discovers itself, but hate it when it discovers them."[12] Although truth continues to operate in spite of this obfuscation, it never coerces people into accepting its principles. Always there to be discovered, truth must be acknowledged and assented to over the many distractions with things other than truth that occupy our lives.[13]

The Christians Did It

Truth came under fire in the aftermath of the Visigoth's sack of Rome in 410. Among the many criticisms the pagans raised against Christians,[14] one stood out for its deviousness. "There you have it, he says, in Christian times Rome is destroyed."[15] This lie was devious because in a factual sense it was mostly true. In flirting with truth it was, by the closeness of its association, well equipped to deceive. Although Rome had been sacked and not taken down entirely, indeed the event had occurred during what many referred to as "Christian times."

For Augustine, the phrase "Christian times" would undergo significant nuancing and reconsideration in the context of his deepening sense of the complex relationship between Rome as a political entity and the progress of the faith over the course of time. Prior to 400, "Christian times" evoked a triumphalism that connected the actions of kings in history with Christianity's subsequent spread and stability.[16] After 400, Robert Markus has shown that the phrase acquired a negative connotation, which had been borrowed from the anti-Christian polemics of an earlier age. "Long before the Sack of Rome in 410 we hear of people complaining about a decline in the felicity of human affairs in 'Christian times,' and in the year 400 Augustine, reporting such complaints, asserts that they derive from the polemical writings of the philosophers."[17] When the phrase appeared again in *City of God* and in sermons preached after the sack of Rome, it was used ironically to rebuke the pagan opposition. The problem was that the majority of people Augustine preached to apparently believed the lie that the "Christian times" had failed somehow to prevent their current suffering in the context of political uncertainty.

The challenge for Augustine was to disengage the factual accuracy of the statement ("in Christian times Rome is destroyed") from its misleading assumption that the "Christian times" were in some way implicated in the Visigoths' attack. Primarily, there were four ways in which this was accomplished. First, Augustine distinguished the "pressures" of the world from its "scandals." The pressures consisted in every kind of physical and mental suffering associated with political instability. It was the ongoing difficulty of living in this fallen world. The scandals were the lies people told to divert Christians from the truth of the faith. They introduced ethical ambiguity where once there had been certainty:

> So here you are, for example, with some influential man asking of you the favor of a little false evidence to assist him in his land-grabbing, in his plunder. You, for your part, refuse; you refuse to lie, in order not to deny the truth. To make a long story short, he gets angry, he is influential, so he pressures you. Your friend comes along, who doesn't like you being pressured, doesn't like you being in trouble. "Please, I beg you, do what he suggests; is it such a big deal?"[18]

Pressures weighed on the flesh, while scandals such as this compromised the integrity of the soul.

Second, Augustine distinguished the brick-and-mortar buildings of Rome, its geographical layout, and physical existence, from the Romans who built it:

> It's human beings who are the pride of a city, human beings who inhabit, plan and govern a city, and they come just to go, are born just to die, come in just to pass on. Heaven and earth will pass away (Matthew 24:35); so why be surprised if a city sometimes comes to an end? And it's possible, of course, that the city's end hasn't come yet; sometime, though, the city's end will come.[19]

Connecting Rome with its inhabitants confirmed that both groups were fated to die a physical death in the world. There was nothing special, in other words, about "Christian times" and, therefore, nothing to blame. Separating the one from the other meant that Rome could perish conceivably without Romans perishing likewise in the death of damnation. To borrow a trope from classical rhetoric, the brick-and-mortar physicality of Rome was not a synecdoche for the people who built it. That was true in spite of the fact that the bodies of the martyrs lay in Rome, filling the city, its physicality, with the assurance of their protection. The disappointment people felt when that protection failed to materialize was palpable: "Rome is suffering such great evils, so where are the memorials of the Apostles?" they asked.[20] Although their bodies remained physically in the city, their promises were not of this world.

Third, the "Christian times" that people argued about were just an illusion. It was true that Rome had been sacked during a time in which a majority of the people and their political structures were Christian. Yet there was no point, according to Augustine, in filling the so-called "times" with the attributes of the people who lived them. "Times" were not Christian, people were. "Evils abound, and God has willed that evils should abound. If only evil people didn't abound, then evils wouldn't abound. The times are evil, the times are troubled, that's what people say. Let us live good lives, and the times are good. We ourselves are the times. Whatever we are like, that's what the times are like."[21] To put it simply, people were responsible for the evil times they lived in. It had nothing to do with Christians failing to honor the pagan gods. And just as "Christian times" did not exist as something tangible to blame, neither did the uniqueness of the evil. Instead of being distinctively Christian, as the pagan critics said, the troubles they faced currently were no different from the troubles of the past. The problem was in the perception that the times they had not experienced were more agreeable somehow than the present times they lived in.[22] Augustine saw it as a matter of transgenerational continuity. Each generation had failed collectively to transmit the magnitude of its suffering.

Finally, Augustine called out the lie that bishops sometimes told to attract crowds into their churches. "Live as you like," they said, "don't worry. God won't destroy anyone as long as you keep the Christian faith. He won't destroy what he has redeemed, he won't destroy those for whom he has shed his blood. And if you want to indulge your spirits at the games, go. What's wrong with it?"[23] This was the insidious lie that led people to believe that signing onto Christ guaranteed their enjoyment of the illusory world they indulged in. It was the lie that absolved Christians of all responsibility for their actions. It was also the lie that made them think they were destined to subvert the world to their selfish desires.

The reality was that ever since the Fall in the garden, humanity and its world were broken. The consequences of the primordial deception were still reverberating throughout the course of history. Deception was still, in some sense, the law of the land, which is why there was no obvious correlation between moral conduct and worldly success. In such a fallen state, it was possible, and even likely, that aligning one's interest according to the same deception under which the world now functioned would lead to material reward. Contrast this with the exercise of virtue, which could be counted on mainly to produce a greater degree of virtue. It was a deception, in fact, to think that a correlation between moral conduct and worldly success existed at all, or that it had been promised uniquely to Christians. Augustine chastised those who were thinking of selecting a wealthy and influential pagan as their patron instead of God.[24] Comparing their own state of misery with the flourishing lives of pagans, such Christians had overassessed the value of material reward.

The truth was sobering. It was more likely in this regard for pagans—those for whom there was no conflict between the deception that continued to operate and the worldly values to which they subscribed—to expect good fortune. To the extent that faith in Christ put Christians into conflict with the structures of the world, they were no longer in a position to benefit directly from its deceptive modes of operation. Apparently, this disappointing truth had been a source of confusion for Augustine's congregations. Many had thought that subscribing to Christ was synonymous with subduing the world. They had confused the abundance of milk and honey promised in the Old Testament with the grace in Christ that it signified in the New.[25] The spiritual error led people back to the servitude of the law with its expectation of material benefits.

> So [the law] bears children for servitude. Who are they? People who serve God for the sake of earthly goods. When they have them they give thanks; when they lack them they blaspheme. Those who serve God for such things cannot serve him truly and from the heart. They look at people who don't serve our God, and they notice they have what they themselves are serving God for, and they say to themselves, "What's the use of my serving God? Have I got as much as that fellow who blasphemes him every day? A man prays and starves; a man blasphemes and belches."[26]

The spiritual error produced unjustified expectations about how they, as newly formed Christians, related to the world that were even more disturbing to their spiritual formation than the initial misunderstanding they had been vulnerable to. By expecting to prosper in line with the power structures of the world, they diverted themselves from the hope that should have abided in Christ. This false alignment with materialism, first, corrupted those who benefited from it and, then, damaged those who were injured.[27] "Corrupted" because the success they gained was built on self-deception, and "injured" because the harm that followed when their luck ran out compromised their spiritual integrity.

Augustine called for a new way of assessing the qualities, attributes, and modes of existence that people deemed important for their flourishing. Such benefits as health, honor, wealth, and family were not the external goods of the Stoic wise man, not the entitlement of those who performed their civic duty, and not the reward owed from God for practicing virtue. They were among the temporal benefits that Christians may or may not acquire while traveling through this life as pilgrims in a strange world. With the knowledge that such things were transitory and their spiritual value uncertain, the Christian was supposed to assess her priorities accordingly. For example, it was often the case that poverty and obscurity were spiritually useful, while wealth and fame were harmful.[28] In the light of this warning, it was acceptable to ask for a temporal benefit, but only in a steady moderation that tempered its potentially damaging effect on spiritual progress.

This meant that Christians were to prioritize long-term spiritual progress over short-sighted happiness, the health of the soul was to outweigh the longing for material success, and temporal advantages were to be distinguished from eternal blessings. With respect to the latter, such benefits as the imperishability and immortality of the flesh and soul, the company of angels, and the heavenly city were among those eternal joys that Christians were supposed to long for persistently. It put them in a continuous state of prayer: "Desire is praying always, even if the tongue is silent. If you desire always, you are praying always. When does prayer go to sleep? When desire grows cold."[29] The reprioritization that Augustine called for placed Christians in correct alignment with God. Because it detached their self-assessment from the values of worldly materialism, it allowed them to persist in praise of God, no matter their circumstances. "Whether it goes well in the flesh, whether it goes poorly in the flesh, I will bless the Lord at all times, his praise always in my mouth."[30]

The logical consequence of this new arrangement was the devaluation of earthly kingdoms in the context of history. For Augustine, the evil times were synonymous with the evil people who failed to align themselves with God. To the extent that people were responsible for the moral quality of the times they lived in, the kingdoms of the world were not a reified abstraction. They were the concrete expression of the people who built them. In the case of Rome, its history, as told by Augustine, was fraught with mythical contradictions. While Romulus founded Rome, it was Aeneas (said Augustine in a literary flourish blending Virgil with the historian Sallust, d. c.35 BCE) who settled the Trojan refugees there, along with their fugitive gods.[31] The uneasy mixing of legend, though, is not the point. It is rather that Rome, a city (civitas) of people founded by men, was flawed from its inception. The same gods that had failed Troy would later fail Rome.

For Augustine, it was fitting somehow that such attenuated gods had been brought to protect a new earthly city, Rome, that was by its nature, just as weak and prone to destruction as the fallen Troy the gods had fled. The uselessness of the gods was appropriate to the transience of the city. Given that the gods the pagans longed for never had the power to protect Rome effectively, there was no imaginable sense in which the failure to sacrifice to them had left the city vulnerable. Rhetorically, the presumed connection between the welfare of the state and the gods it sacrificed to had been broken.

Augustine adduced numerous historical examples, as in *City of God* book 3, to make the point. One such case from a sermon he preached in approximately 411, just after the sack of Rome, will suffice here. We are told that only a few years earlier Rhadagaisus, the King of the Goths, had marched on Rome with a large army (consisting of around 20,000 men). Devoted to the god Jupiter, he was known to make daily sacrifices. By that time, however, the pagan statues in the city of Rome had been demolished already. People interpreted the Gothic occupation under the leadership of this devout man as an obvious rebuke by the gods for their own inability to sacrifice. "Look, we are not sacrificing, this man is sacrificing, so we who are not allowed to sacrifice have to be conquered by someone who sacrifices."[32] Augustine reminded them that Rhadagaisus had been defeated (by the Vandal general Stilicho, d. 408), in spite of his devotion to the gods, whereas Rome had been spared, for a while at least, from destruction. The logic of the gods' inertness worked both ways. The current situation involved the Arian Goths who had marched on Rome under the direction of their king, Alaric.[33] Opposed to idol worship, they succeeded, nonetheless, in conquering those who longed to revive the city's sacrifice to its fallen gods. The conclusion to be drawn was that ritual sacrifice had no influence on the welfare of the state.

Though detached from pagan ritual, the suffering that people experienced in earthly kingdoms over the course of time served a spiritual purpose. It educated them in, and made them tolerant of, the vicissitudes of misfortune.[34] Augustine compared such worldly tribulation to the mechanical operation of an oil press. When put under the pressure of a special apparatus, the seeds from fruits and nuts expel the oil that is prized, while the rest of the raw materials, the dregs, are separated and then discarded. Following the logic of the metaphor, famine, war, poverty, and disease are among the pressures that kingdoms apply, whereas the people are the seeds. Pressed by the miseries of life, they are free to become either the oil or the dregs. They choose the former when they praise God in spite of their current tribulation, and the latter when they complain of the evil they must endure in the context of "Christian times."

For Augustine, suffering could also be therapeutic, in the sense that the so-called "tribulations of history" followed a method of spiritual refinement and education similar to that of the "good physician." In both cases, pain is applied to treat a deeper, more insidious wound, the pain of corporate suffering, on the one hand, and the pain of individual affliction, on the other. The physician knows when to remove a limb so rotten that it would infect the entire body if it were permitted to remain. Similarly, God knows when it is time to let the material structures of earthly kingdoms— for example, its amphitheaters—fall into ruin in order to make their felt absence serve as a spiritual correction.

The educational and therapeutic value Augustine attributed to suffering placed the apparently endless adversities Christians were experiencing in a new moral framework. On its surface, everyone seemed to be suffering the same hardships as a result of the Gothic occupation. The difference had to do with the outcome of that suffering and the quality of the person who experienced it. "What is important is not the sort of things that are suffered, but the sort of person who suffers them."[35] Those who were committed to developing their virtue emerged from tribulation with their faith intact, while the rest confirmed their spiritual condemnation by digging themselves more deeply into the hole of their rebellion.

This observation refines the statements I made in Chapter 3, where Christians and pagans were said to have suffered alike simply because Christians had been unwilling to criticize those in power whom they knew to be corrupt.[36] They preferred their personal security and happiness to the harm that might come to them if they told the truth. In making that decision, they showed themselves to love the same worldly materialism as the unjust power brokers they failed to call out. In other words, their nonintervention was "the result of the bonds (*vincula*) of selfishness, not the duties (*officia*) of love."[37] When interpreted in the light of the educational and therapeutic value of suffering, it is clear that the refusal by Christians to let go of the world explains why they were being spiritually disciplined by its trials. This material world chastised, punished, and corrected those who were willing, first, to see themselves as tarnished by and, then, to remove themselves from its various modes of operation. There was, in other words, a redemptive value to the pain.

The sack of Rome had produced, nonetheless, the material conditions under which Christians suffered the same distress as their pagan counterparts for their compliance with this corrupt world. No matter the spiritual benefits of suffering, there was the overwhelming sense of unfairness among Christians. It seemed that their failure as Christians was just the failure to stand up to the dishonesty and immorality of the state. "This seems to be no small reason why the good are oppressed with the wicked, when God is pleased to punish corrupt morals with the suffering of temporal punishments. For they are punished together, not because they lead a wicked life together, but because they love this present life, not, to be sure, equally, but nevertheless together."[38] In the light of this corporate system of justice, in which the so-called "good and wicked" endured the same "temporal punishments," questions about the nature and limits of freedom were raised acutely. How free are we really in a corrupt and immoral state, if we can be punished temporally for things we did not do, but benefited from indirectly? In addition to human freedom, the question also concerns the relationship between individual and corporate identity.

Undeserved Suffering

Such questions set the stage for understanding the meaning of the controversy with Pelagius (d. 418), the monk from Britain who fled to North Africa to escape ill-treatment by the Visigoths. Concerned about the moral degradation of society, Pelagius believed that a rigorous asceticism inspired by grace made the individual pleasing to God in a way that contributed to his or her salvation. In contrast with Augustine, he deemphasized the extent to which grace helped restructure fallen human nature according to a new set of divinely shaped priorities. While Pelagius accused Augustine of compromising the freedom of our will, Augustine accused Pelagius of denying the operation of grace and, thereby, placing us in spiritual servitude:

We do not deny free choice. Rather, if the Son sets you free, the truth says, then you will truly be free. You begrudge this deliverer to those captives to whom you attribute a false freedom. After all, one becomes a slave, as scripture says, to one's conqueror.

And no one is set free from this chain of slavery, from which no human being is exempt, except by the grace of the deliverer.[39]

For Augustine, freedom consists in faith in God and in the truth of Christ, not in the efforts of the individual.

Scholars have shown that the main lines of Augustine's theology of grace, free will, and the Fall had been articulated prior to his arguments with Pelagius.[40] We can assume, therefore, that the intensity of the debate was driven by something other than the need to refine doctrine. It was driven by, among other things,[41] the challenge of understanding the apparent injustice of individual and corporate suffering in the context of the impersonal forces of political transformation. To the extent that Christians are punished temporally for things they cannot control, they are not, and never will be, free. Without "the Son setting them free," they remain in servitude to the depravity and corruption of the state, in addition to their individual moral failings. Augustine realized that Pelagianism, with its faith in individual freedom and self-assertion, simply could not work in such a fallen world.

The political turmoil caused by the sack of Rome raised questions about what did, and did not, count as a virtue. For instance, Augustine recalled that certain persons had protected their possessions vigorously from confiscation by the Visigoths. Inspired by materialism, such acts were simply wrong. For Pelagius, in contrast, these were acts of courage that exemplified virtue. Augustine explained the matter like this: virtue was to be distinguished from vice not by the action itself, but by its end:[42]

> Or do you want to say that the greedy have true virtues, when they prudently seek the paths of gain, when they courageously endure many hardships and difficulties to acquire money, when they temperately and soberly chastise their various desires for living a lavish life, when they hold themselves back from the property of others and regard as nothing the loss of their own—which seems to pertain to justice—so that they do not lose more on quarrels and trials?[43]

For something to count as a virtue, it was not enough to look at what was done, but to ask why it was done. The motivation for the action determined its moral quality.

The controversy with Pelagius about the nature of virtue and vice also addressed deep-seated concerns about the operation of justice in the world. Augustine needed to account for the fact that pagans sometimes exhibited virtue that appeared to be true. For example, the Roman statesman Gaius Fabricius Luscinus (c. 3rd century BCE) was known for his moral character. Upheld as a model of virtue, he was less dishonest than Catiline (c. 1st century BCE), the Roman senator who attempted to overthrow the Republic. For Augustine, "Fabricius was less wicked than Catiline, not because he had true virtues, but because he had not strayed very far from true virtues."[44] Fabricius, like the other great families of Rome, had exemplified the civic virtues that were meant to serve either "demons or human glory." In the progress of their fortune, there were slight and sporadic connections to be drawn between the exercise of civic virtue and the enjoyment of material success.[45] Yet the only concrete thing that emerged from the demon gods they served and the honors they chased after was a truncated form of justice that always fell short of the justice of God.

For Augustine, no matter how virtuous we are, perfect justice can never be attained until the eschatological reality of the city of God, where our piety "awaits as its reward in the fellowship of saints, not only human, but also angelic, this, 'that God may be all in all.'"[46] Although the city of God is a distant hope and not of this realm, there are those here presently who live by its principles. They are the "strangers in a strange land," the sojourners, who, for all practical purposes, are in the world, but are not beholden somehow to its mechanisms. Their life in the earthly realm can seem like a contradiction, to the extent that they both repudiate and benefit gently from the power structures of the world. Their skill consists in knowing how to use such material advantages without being seduced by them and diverted from God. The perils of this existence had been stated already in Scripture: "Beloved, I urge you as sojourners and exiles to abstain from the passions of the flesh, which wage war against your soul" (1 Pet. 2:11). "But now they desire a better country, that is a heavenly one" (Heb. 11:16).

On the outside, the sojourners do not look all that different from the rest of the population. They may be wealthy or poor. They may be more or less virtuous. They may work side by side with their earthly counterparts. Rather than a distinct enclave, they are an integrated subset of the earthly city, distinguished from their peers by the object of their love and by the manner in which they relate to the advantages of the world. "The perfection of the Pilgrim City is correspondingly a perfect obedience. It is open to all the rational creation by virtue of their freedom to choose whom to love."[47] Whereas the earthly city is driven by the love of self, the part of the heavenly city that sojourns on earth is driven by the love of God. Whereas the earthly city uses power and wealth to accomplish its ends, the heavenly city puts up with power and wealth to the extent necessary to live on earth. Whereas the one indulges its urges and impulses, the other exhibits an easy restraint. As separate as these two groups are, there is no particular institution to which the heavenly sojourner belongs. "No identification of either of the two cities with any institution or with any empirically definable body of people can be reconciled with this radical dichotomy. Membership of the two cities is mutually exclusive, and there can be no possible overlap."[48]

This mutual exclusivity ensures that the heavenly city will be locked in conflict with its earthly counterpart until the end time. Under the conditions of spiritual warfare, the members of the heavenly city must not be lulled into satisfaction by the material ease of their lives, for there can be no accommodation to the structures and institutions of the earthly realm: "it has come to pass that it is not possible [for the heavenly city] to have common laws of religion with the earthly city, which is why [the heavenly city] necessarily has to dissent from these matters and become burdensome to those who think differently, bearing the brunt of their anger, hatred, and persecution."[49] To the extent that unity is not an option, a diversity of nations, peoples, and languages must coexist without concern for the differences in custom, laws, and institutions. All such things may be used legitimately to secure an earthly peace as long as the final desire rests in God. Relevant here is the well-known distinction Augustine made between the enjoyment of something for its own sake (*frui*) and the use (*uti*) of it to obtain something else.[50] We are to use, not enjoy, this material existence, because we are to find our spiritual fulfillment elsewhere.

Although the dichotomy between the two cities has consequences in the material realm, its certainty is not fully realized until the final judgment. Prior to that time, the cities remain interconnected, and the principles of worldly power continue to operate. To the extent the cities remain intermingled, they are in a state of spiritual warfare that need not manifest in the physical plane. This inherent tension does not always function to the detriment of the heavenly sojourners. Because their objectives are different, they make different use of the same worldly materials at their disposal:

> And these two cities are meanwhile mingled, at the end to be separated; against each other mutually in conflict, the one for iniquity, the other for righteousness, the one for deception, the other for truth. And sometimes this very temporal mingling brings it to pass that certain men belonging to the city Babylon manage affairs regarding Jerusalem, and again certain men belonging to Jerusalem manage affairs regarding Babylon.[51]

Obligated to the underlying principles of their overlapping structures, the two cities cannot be differentiated by the actions of people working on their behalf. As long as both cities remain in the world—the earthly city on its own terms and the heavenly city as a sojourner—there will be no complete separation.

The corporate body known as the heavenly city is really just a group of individuals that has subordinated their will to God in love. The same principles that govern the individual's moral choices, and determine their moral value, also apply to the heavenly city. What makes an action count as a virtue is its motivation, not simply its moral quality. The same orientation toward love and moral ends determines the membership of the heavenly city. This should not be confused with the conceit of individual self-sufficiency that Augustine put to rest in the Pelagian controversy. Any such confidence in the capacity of the will to flourish under its own power already had been dismissed as unwarranted. As Rowan Williams has remarked, "the anti-Pelagian works ... [repudiate] any idea that we could take as a theological starting point an individual will seeking to make peace with God."[52]

Virtue or Worldly Success?

For Augustine, the controversy with Pelagius raised the question of how, exactly, Christians were supposed to live amid the corruption of this earthly realm. For Pelagius, the answer had to do with the effort of the individual to rise above his limits toward a perfection of his own making. I have suggested that this theology simply could not work in the light of the Visigoths' invasion. To the extent that Christians suffered alongside pagans, there was no plausible way for Pelagius to explain the perception of injustice. Just as righteousness accrued by faith, not works, there was no reliable connection between the exercise of virtue and worldly success.

Whereas for Pelagius, the motivation behind the deed had little moral significance, for Augustine, the motivation of the individual was synonymous with the deed and determined its moral value. This is where his moral psychology comes into play. In elevating such emotions as grief and compassion to the level of a virtue, Augustine made them relevant to the moral lives of those who sojourned in the earthly realm. Intertwined with human action, emotions are the truth that Christians tell and the inspiration that stimulate them to perform charitable deeds. Augustine's definition of compassion bears repeating here: "What is compassion except a kind of sympathy in our heart for the suffering of another that surely compels us to help as much as we can?" In their lower form, emotions drag us down. But when they are ordered correctly, they help realign our interests and clarify our moral priorities. "For instance, anger with a sinner to correct him, sadness for someone distressed to relieve him, fear for someone in danger that he not perish."[53] Emotions accommodate our fallen nature to the harshness of the world. Whereas the angels do not need emotions in order to act compassionately, for us they are a necessary adaptation, "So long as we wear the infirmity of this life, we are rather worse people than better if we have none of these emotions at all."[54] By connecting us to other people's suffering, our emotions neutralize the impulse toward narcissism and human exploitation. Without their benevolent provocation, we are led complacently into self-deception.

Along with Augustine, we may conclude that emotions are a provisional way of managing and prioritizing our moral commitments in the context of this broken world. From the book of Genesis he knew that sadness and sorrow were not intrinsic to creation, but came into the world only after the Fall.[55] God created the first man, Adam, with a blameless nature that was free from the malignant passions.[56] It was Adam who then used the gift of his free will to corrupt this nature and make himself bad. For Augustine, the problem with Pelagianism could be summed up like this: "When man was good he couldn't keep himself good, and now that he is bad, is he going to make himself good?"[57] Even with the moral benefits that accrue from such good emotions as compassion, there is no way for people to generate their salvation by their efforts.

The challenges posed by Pelagius joined with the challenges posed by the widespread perception of unjust suffering to force Augustine's hand. Hard questions about the limits of virtue and of human accountability had to be answered. "If a pagan were to clothe the naked, would it be a sin, because it does not come from faith?"[58] For Pelagius, the answer was "no," but for Augustine, it was certainly "yes." "Without faith it is not possible to please God," he said, quoting Hebrews 11:6. What about such apparently benevolent emotions as mercy and compassion, and the charitable deeds that followed; are these not always good? For Augustine, the line had been drawn in the sand. Even emotions that were apparently virtuous could be sinful if there was no faith in the feeling:

> If it is a defect to be merciful in a bad manner, it is undoubtedly a defect to be merciful without faith. But if mercy by itself with its natural compassion is a good act, one who practices it without faith makes a bad use of this good, and one who acts without faith does this good act in a bad manner, and one who does something in a bad manner surely sins.[59]

There was no possibility for true virtue among pagans. That being the case, there was also no reason to assume that Christians who had suffered amid the Visigothic invasion did so because they were morally inferior in every way. It was not a question of the number or even the quality of the virtuous acts that had been performed. There were rather several additional factors that contributed to their suffering: first, there was the complacency among Christians who failed to live as sojourners in this fallen world; second, there was the collective suffering that resulted from joint participation in the benefits of living in a corrupt and deceptive commonwealth; and finally, there was the possibility that even Christians had performed seemingly virtuous actions without the mindset of faith.

Overcoming the Finite

The implicit connection Augustine draws between faith and feeling says a great deal about how we are supposed to live in this material realm. Seemingly virtuous acts, including acts of compassion and mercy, when performed without faith become, in his view, sins because they bind us to the logic of the world. This is the logic of finitude, where the consequences of our actions are limited to what we can see and where the satisfaction of desire is the measure of our flourishing. In the purely ethical system that Pelagius envisioned, the interior life of the person has little to do with the quality of his or her moral actions. As long as the actions are true, he or she need not have any particular orientation to the finite things of this world.

Augustine's emotional life had taught him otherwise. How we orient ourselves with respect to the finite determines how we orient ourselves with respect to God. This is what he meant when he wrote about the emptiness he had felt when his friend died. He had loved his friend in the context of the finite, for what they had shared, for the places they had frequented, for the program that played over in his mind of their many conversations. When all this ended, he experienced the shock of recollection as overwhelming loss. Decades later he came to realize that he had loved something mortal as if it would never die. In the process of this self-deception, he had lost forever what he could have loved eternally in the context of Christ. He never revealed the name of his friend because the friendship had vanished amid the finite limitations of the world he inhabited.

For Augustine, the logic of finitude is overcome in Abraham's binding of Isaac, a story of faith, resignation, and fear. Recall that God commanded the patriarch Abraham to offer his only son Isaac as a sacrifice. In obedience, Abraham bound his son to the altar, at which point an angel intervened and stopped the sacrifice. Having demonstrated his fear of God to God's satisfaction, Abraham was permitted to sacrifice a lamb in place of his son. For the early Christians, the episode prefigured God's sacrifice of his only-begotten son, Christ. Augustine was consistent, in this regard, with those who interpreted the story before him. What is distinctive about Augustine is the conceptual leap he takes into paradox: "Therefore the pious father, faithfully keeping this promise which had to be fulfilled through this son whom God commanded to be killed, did not doubt that he whom he assumed he would never receive would

be restored to him when he had offered him up."[60] The faith of
Abraham did not reinforce the linear logic of the wishful thought
that God would stop the sacrifice. It overcame the logic of the finite
and resigned him to the untold possibility of the infinite. In every
fiber of his being, Abraham knew—somehow, inexplicably—that he
could sacrifice his son and have him restored to him forever.

There are certain affinities with Søren Kierkegaard's (d. 1855)
interpretation of the same. Like Augustine, Kierkegaard saw in the
binding of Isaac a repudiation of the logic of the finite for something
far more spiritually transformative. Kierkegaard makes explicit,
however, what Augustine gently hints at, namely the possibility of
the absurd breaking into this realm. For Kierkegaard, the paradox
of Abraham's faith resides in the knowledge that he can both
sacrifice Isaac and have him present in the now. In this regard,
Abraham exemplifies what Kierkegaard calls "the knight of faith,"
someone who appears to be an ordinary man immersed in the daily
grind of the world he inhabits. With careful attention to detail, such
a man minds his business and pays his taxes, while delighting in
unremarkable pleasures. As the knight of faith, he does not have the
detached strangeness or air of superiority of his predecessor along
this spiritual journey, the so-called "knight of infinite resignation."
He does not function like this other knight, who resigns himself
to the presence of the infinite in the realm of the finite. Rather, the
knight of faith continually makes "the movement of infinity," which
always brings him back to finitude, without so much as missing a
step.[61] "[H]e has felt the pain of renouncing everything, whatever
is most precious in the world, and yet to him finitude tastes just
as good as to one who has never known anything higher."[62] Like
Abraham, his resignation to the "untold possibility of the infinite"
lets him live out the paradox of the absurd.

For Augustine, Abraham's binding of Isaac is not a straightforward
lesson about the delayed gratification that comes from postponing
Isaac's return until the afterlife. Nor is its significance limited to the
logical absurdity of losing Isaac, while simultaneously having him
too. It is also about the value we assign to the goods of this world,
whether health, wealth, honor, or family.[63] Isaac meant everything
to Abraham, and yet God asked him to accept, and perhaps even
revel in, the prospect of unimaginable loss. I have already shown
how the Stoics tried to relativize even such a highly valued good as
this one to the tranquility of the wise man, whose individual virtue

was treasured above all other goods. Augustine saw the limitations of such an ethical system. Its promise of equanimity did not allow for compassionate engagement with the sorrows of the world. Nor did the confidence in ascetic achievement that Pelagius had proposed. Neither moral framework could respond adequately to the experience of unjust suffering. The Stoics failed because they did not commit emotionally to other people's pain, and Pelagius, because he did not make the spiritual move into the uncertainty of the infinite. In joining faith with virtue, Augustine makes this move into a spiritual plane where feeling and faith transform ordinary deeds of civic commitment into Christian virtues.

Sorrow is the human condition that Christ assumed in order to heal our fallen nature. The richness of the emotional life that Augustine described, first, connects us compassionately with the same suffering that Christ assumed and, then, urges us to live that relationship out in the context of this finite world. Like the knight of faith, we resign ourselves to the "deep sorrow of existence," while knowing the "bliss of infinity."[64]

Notes

1   August., *C. acad.*, 1.8.23. See trans. Peter King, *Augustine: Against the Academics* and *The Teacher* (Indianapolis, IN: Hackett Publishing Company, 1995).

2   August., *De beat. vit.*, 2.13–14.

3   See, for example, August., *De Trin.*, 15.12.21.

4   Blake D. Dutton, *Augustine and Academic Skepticism: A Philosophical Study* (Ithaca, NY: Cornell University Press, 2016), 49.

5   August., *De civ. D.*, 11.26.

6   Ibid.

7   Ibid.

8   Ibid.

9   August., *C. acad.*, 1.2.5.26–30.

10 August., *Retract.*, 1.1.4; see also 1 Pet. 4:6.

11 See generally, August., *De Gen. c. Man.*, 2.1.2.

12 August., *Conf.*, 10.23; adapted slightly from trans. Watts, *Confessions*, 139.

13 Ibid.

14 See Chapter 3, above.

15 August., *Serm.*, 81.9.
16 Robert A. Markus, *Saeculum: History and Society in the Theology of St. Augustine* (Cambridge: Cambridge University Press, 1970), 32.
17 Ibid. 37.
18 August., *Serm.*, 81.4, adapted slightly from trans. Hill, *Sermons* 3/3, 361.
19 August., *Serm.*, 46.8, adapted slightly from trans. Hill, *Sermons* 3/2, 267.
20 August., *Serm.*, 296.5.6; adapted slightly from trans. Hill, *Sermons* 3/8, 206.
21 August., *Serm.*, 80.8; trans. Hill, *Sermons* 3/3, 355–356.
22 August., *Serm.*, 25.3.
23 August., Serm., 46.8; trans. Hill, *Sermons* 3/2, 267.
24 August., *Serm.*, 33A.3.
25 August., *Serm.*, 25.1–2.
26 August., *Serm.*, 25.2; trans. Hill, *Sermons* 3/2, 83.
27 Augustine says this explicitly in *Serm.*, 46.10; trans. Hill, *Sermons* 3/2, 269.
28 August., *Serm.*, 80.7.
29 Ibid. adapted slightly from trans. Hill, *Sermons* 3/3, 355.
30 August., *Serm.*, 105.8; see trans. Hill, *Sermons* 3/4, 92.
31 August., *Serm.*, 81.9.
32 August., *Serm.*, 105.13; see trans. Hill, *Sermons* 3/4, 95.
33 Note that Alaric's army included 12,000 of Rhadagaisus' men, who, after their defeat, had been drafted into the Roman army. See Peter J. Heather, *The Fall of the Roman Empire: A New History of Rome and the Barbarians* (Oxford: Oxford University Press, 2006), 197–8.
34 See August., *Serm.*, 105.13.
35 August., *De civ. D.*, 1.8.
36 See also August., *Serm.*, 25.4, where even the just are criticized.
37 August., *De civ. D.*, 1.9.
38 Ibid; trans. McCracken, *The City of God*, 45.
39 August., *De nupt. et conc.*, 2.3.8; see also August., *C. Iul.*, 4.21; trans., Roland J. Teske, S. J., *Answer to the Pelagians* 2 (New York: New City Press, 1998), 57.
40 Carol Harrison, *Christian Truth and Fractured Humanity* (Oxford: Oxford University Press, 2000), 113–14.
41 Ibid. 106–114.
42 August., *C. Iul.*, 4.21; trans. Teske, *Pelagians* 2, 393.
43 August., *C. Iul.*, 4.19; trans. Teske, *Pelagians* 2, 391.
44 August., *C. Iul.*, 4.25; trans. Teske, *Pelagians* 2, 395.
45 See, August., *De civ. D.*, 2.23.

46   Ibid. 14.28; trans. Levine, *The City of God*, 407.
47   Miles Hollingworth, *Pilgrim City: St. Augustine of Hippo and His Innovation in Political Thought* (London: T&T Clark, 2010), 190.
48   Markus, *Saeculum*, 60.
49   August., *De civ. D.*, 19.17.
50   August., *De doct. Christ.*, 1.3–4.
51   August., *En. in Ps.*, 61.8; see 62.4, Augustine, *Expositions on the Book of Psalms*, 441.
52   Williams, *On Augustine*, 30.
53   August., *De civ. D.*, 9.5.
54   Ibid. 14.9.
55   August., *De Gen. c. Man.*, 2.1.2.
56   August., *De Gen. ad lit.* 14.23–24; Wetzel, "Augustine," 357.
57   August., *Serm.*, 26.3; trans. Hill, *Sermons* 3/2, 94.
58   August., *C. Iul.*, 4.30; trans. Teske, *Pelagians* 2, 398.
59   August., *C. Iul.*, 4.31; trans. Teske, *Pelagians* 2, 399.
60   August., *De civ. D.*, 16.32; see trans., Dods, *The City of God*, 329.
61   Søren Kierkegaard, *Fear and Trembling* (London: Penguin Books, 2003), 70.
62   Ibid. 69–70.
63   See Kevin Hoffman, "Facing Threats to Earthly Felicity: A Reading of Kierkegaard's *Fear and Trembling*," *Journal of Religious Ethics* 34, no. 3 (2006): 439–59 (442–3).
64   Kierkegaard, *Fear and Trembling*, 69.

BIBLIOGRAPHY

Annas, Julia. "Aristotle on Memory and the Self." *Oxford Studies in Ancient Philosophy* 4 (1986): 99–117.

Arbesmann, O. S. A., Rudolph. "The Concept of 'Christus Medicus' in St. Augustine." *Traditio* 10 (1954): 1–28.

Archambault, Paul J. "Augustine, Memory, and the Development of Autobiography." *Augustinian Studies* 13 (1982): 23–30.

Barret, Lee C. *Eros and Self-Emptying: The Intersections of Augustine and Kierkegaard.* Grand Rapids, MI: William B. Eerdman's Publishing Company, 2013.

Bavel, Tarsicius J. van. *Recherches sur la Christologie de Saint Augustin. L'humain et le divin dans le Christ d'après Saint Augustin.* Fribourg: University Press of Fribourg, 1954.

BeDuhn, Jason David. *Augustine's Manichaean Dilemma, vol. 1: Conversion and Apostasy, 373–388 AD.* Philadelphia: University of Pennsylvania Press, 2010.

BeDuhn, Jason David. *The Manichaean Body in Discipline and Ritual.* Baltimore, MD: Johns Hopkins University Press, 2000.

Boyd, Richard. "Pity's Pathologies Portrayed: Rousseau and the Limits of Democratic Compassion." *Political Theory* 32, no. 4 (2004): 519–46.

Brachtendorf, Johannes. "Cicero and Augustine on the Passions." *Revues des Études Augustiniennes* 43 (1997): 289–308.

Breyfogle, Todd. "Memory and the Imagination in Augustine's Confessions." *New Blackfriars* 75, no. 881 (1994): 210–23.

Brown, Peter. *Augustine of Hippo: A Biography* [first published 1967]. Berkeley: University of California Press, 2000.

Byers, Sarah Catherine. *Perception, Sensibility, and Moral Motivation in Augustine: A Stoic-Platonic Synthesis.* Cambridge: Cambridge University Press, 2013.

Byers, Sarah Catherine. "The Psychology of Compassion: Stoicism in City of God 9.5." In *A Companion to Augustine.* Edited by Mark Vessey, 130–48. Oxford: Wiley-Blackwell, 2012.

Canning, Raymond. "Augustine on the Identity of the Neighbour and the Meaning of True Love for Him 'as ourselves' (Matt. 22.39) and 'as Christ has loved us' (Jn. 13.34)." *Augustiniana* 36 (1986): 161–239.

Ceulemans, Anne-Emmanuelle. "Instruments Real and Imaginary: Aaron's Interpretation of Isidore and an Illustrated Copy of the Toscanello." In *Early Music History*, vol. 21. Edited by Iain Fenlon, 1–26. Cambridge: Cambridge University Press, 2002.

Clark, Gillian, "Caritas: Augustine on Love and Fellow-Feeling." In *Hope, Joy, and Affection in the Classical World*. Edited by Ruth R. Caston and Robert A. Kaster, 209–25. New York: Oxford University Press, 2016.

Colish, Marcia L. *The Stoic Tradition from Antiquity to the Early Middle Ages*, vol. 1. Leiden: Brill, 1990.

Davies, Oliver. *A Theology of Compassion: Metaphysics of Difference and the Renewal of Tradition*. London: SCM Press, 2001.

Didion, Joan. *The Year of Magical Thinking*. New York: A. A. Knopf, 2005.

Doody, John, Kim Paffenroth, and Helene Tallon Russell, eds. *Augustine and Kierkegaard*. Lanham, MD: Lexington Books, 2017.

Drobner, Hubertus R. *Person-Exegese und Christologie bei Augustinus: zur Herkunft der Formel Una Persona*. Leiden: Brill, 1986.

Dusen, David van. *Space of Time: Sensualist Interpretation of Time in Augustine, Confessions 10 to 12*. Leiden: Brill, 2014.

Dutton, Blake D. *Augustine and Academic Skepticism: A Philosophical Study*. Ithaca, NY: Cornell University Press, 2016.

Ferngren, Gary B. *Medicine and Health Care in Early Christianity*. Baltimore, MD: Johns Hopkins University Press, 2009.

Forman-Barzilai, Fonna. "Sympathy in Spaces: Adam Smith on Proximity." *Political Theory* 33, no. 2 (2005): 189–217.

Fox, Robin Lane. *Augustine: Conversions to Confessions*. New York: Basic Books, 2015.

Gardner, Iain, and Samuel N. C. Lieu. *Manichaean Texts from the Roman Empire*. Cambridge: Cambridge University Press, 2004.

Harrison, Carol. *Christian Truth and Fractured Humanity*. Oxford: Oxford University Press, 2000.

Heather, Peter J. *The Fall of the Roman Empire: A New History of Rome and the Barbarians*. Oxford: Oxford University Press, 2006.

Hedrick, Charles W. *History and Silence: Purge and Rehabilitation of Memory in Late Antiquity*. Austin: University of Texas Press, 2000.

Hochschild, Paige E. *Memory in Augustine's Theological Anthropology*. Oxford: Oxford University Press, 2012.

Hoffman, Kevin. "Facing Threats to Earthly Felicity: A Reading of Kierkegaard's *Fear and Trembling*." *Journal of Religious Ethics* 34, no. 3 (2006): 439–59.

Hollingworth, Miles. *Pilgrim City: St. Augustine of Hippo and His Innovation in Political Thought*. London: T&T Clark, 2010.

Hollingworth, Miles. *Saint Augustine of Hippo: An Intellectual Biography*. Oxford: Oxford University Press, 2013.

Kelsey, Morton T. *Healing and Christianity: In Ancient Thought and Modern Times*. London: SCM Press, 1973.

Kierkegaard, Søren. *Fear and Trembling*. London: Penguin Books, 2003.

Koller, Alice. *Stations of Solitude*. New York: Morrow, 1990.

Lambert, David. "The Uses of Decay: History in Salvian's *De Gubernatione Dei*." In *History, Apocalypse, and the Secular Imagination: New Essays on Augustine's City of God*. Edited by Mark Vessey and Karla Pollmann, 115–30. Bowling Green, OH: Philosophy Documentation Center, 1999.

Lancel, Serge. *St. Augustine*. London: SCM Press, 2002.

Lössl, Josef. "Augustine's Confessions as a Consolation of Philosophy." In *In Search of Truth: Augustine, Manichaeism, and Other Gnosticism*. Edited by Jacob Albert van Den Berg, Annemaré Kotzé, Tobias Nicklas, and Madeline Scopelio, 47–73. Leiden: Brill, 2011.

Markus, Robert A. *Saeculum: History and Society in the Theology of St. Augustine*. Cambridge: Cambridge University Press, 1970.

Mirguet, Françoise. *An Early History of Compassion: Emotion and Imagination in Hellenistic Judaism*. Cambridge: Cambridge University Press, 2017.

Mirguet, Françoise. "Emotional Responses to the Pain of Others in Josephus's Rewritten Scriptures and the Testament of Zebulun: Between Power and Vulnerability." *Journal of Biblical Literature* 133, no. 4 (2014): 838–57.

Nouwen, Henri J. M., Donald P. McNeill, and Douglas A. Morrison. *Compassion: A Reflection on the Christian Life*. New York and London: Doubleday, 1982.

Nussbaum, Martha C. *Upheavals of Thought: The Intelligence of Emotions*. Cambridge: Cambridge University Press, 2001.

Parkin, Anneliese. "'You Do Him No Service': An Exploration of Pagan Almsgiving." In *Poverty in the Roman World*. Edited by Margaret Atkins and Robin Osborne, 60–82. Cambridge: Cambridge University Press, 2006.

Pelikan, Jaroslav. *The Mystery of Continuity: Time and History, Memory and Eternity in the Thought of St. Augustine*. Charlottesville: University Press of Virginia, 1986.

Powell, Samuel M. *The Impassioned Life: Reason and Emotion in the Christian Tradition*. Minneapolis, MN: Fortress Press, 2016.

Ross, Donald L. "Time, the Heaven of Heavens, and Memory in Augustine's *Confessions*." *Augustinian Studies* 22 (1991): 191–205.

Silva, D. A. de. "Ambrose's Use of 4 Maccabees in De Jacob et Vita Beata." *Journal of Early Christian Studies* 22, no. 2 (2014): 287–93.

Smith, Zadie. *NW*. New York: Penguin Press, 2012.

Wessel, Susan. *Passion and Compassion in Early Christianity*. Cambridge: Cambridge University Press, 2016.

Wetzel, James. "Augustine." In *The Oxford Handbook of Religion and Emotion*. Edited by John Corrigan, 349–63. Oxford: Oxford University Press, 2008.

Wetzel, James. *Augustine and the Limits of Virtue*. Cambridge: Cambridge University Press, 1992.

Williams, Rowan. "Augustine and the Psalms." *Interpretation* 58 (2004): 17–27.

Williams, Rowan. *On Augustine*. London: Bloomsbury, 2016.

Winn, Robert E. "Revisiting the Date of Authorship of Basil of Caesarea's *Ad Adolescentes*." *The Greek Orthodox Theological Review* 44 (1999): 291–307.

INDEX

www.ingramcontent.com/pod-product-compliance
Ingram Content Group UK Ltd.
Pitfield, Milton Keynes, MK11 3LW, UK
UKHW020736280225
455688UK00012B/682